DIABETIC AIR FRYER COOKBOOK

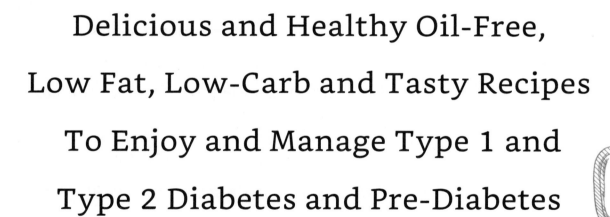

Delicious and Healthy Oil-Free, Low Fat, Low-Carb and Tasty Recipes To Enjoy and Manage Type 1 and Type 2 Diabetes and Pre-Diabetes

Mark Spencer

Table of Contents

Introduction

Twenty years ago, the global estimate of diabetes prevalence in the adolescence to 80 years old age range was around 150 million, and today that number tripled.

Diabetes is a long-term severe chronic disease that occurs when a high level of glucose is in a person's blood. This happens because their body cannot produce any or enough of the hormone insulin or cannot efficiently use the insulin.

Insulin is the hormone produced by the pancreas that allows glucose to enter cells and its consequent use as an energy source. When this mechanism is altered, glucose accumulates in the bloodstream.

Among the United States population, over 34.2 million have diabetes.

Fortunately, every day more and more research is being conducted to help find treatments for this condition.

The symptoms by which you can recognize diabetes can be easily overlooked, and in some situations, they are completely missing.

Most of symptoms are: frequent urination, sudden weight loss, prolonged fatigue, intense hunger, blurred vision, excessive thirst, frequent urination. Studies have shown that participants who are using an air fryer-based diet were able to lower their levels of A1C, a long-term marker of blood glucose control, by 5%.

It should not come as a surprise that a diet of air fryer-cooked meals can lower blood sugar levels; cooking in an air fryer causes fat cells that contain toxins to leak out of the food or into the cooking oil. Even though this oil will need to be disposed of, it will help get rid of some of the excess toxins our bodies take in from unclean food. In addition, by reducing fat cells in our bodies, we don't only lose weight, but we also reduce insulin resistance. This is beneficial because overweight and obese people are at higher risk for developing diabetes than people with normal weights that are following a balanced and healthy lifestyle.

A recent study showed that participants who followed a plant-based diet saw their glucose levels drop dramatically. These results are interesting because, in order to lose weight, most people would need to increase the amount of exercise they perform. A combination of diet and exercise is considered the best way to lose and control weight. Still these participants did not exercise that much more than an average person, they still saw their glucose levels drop significantly. This shows that a good diet can reduce insulin resistance in many people who might not be seeing positive results from exercising or following a different diet.

A plant-based diet or balanced diet also has added benefits because it is rich in phytochemicals, antioxidants, and fiber that can help manage diabetes naturally. These compounds are found in vegetables and other plant-based foods. However, people following this diet might not get enough protein. That is why it is important to include fish, eggs, or legumes (including beans) as part of a balanced diet. These foods can help balance out a meal and ensure you get the recommended protein intake every day.

It has also been proven that whole grains can help lower your risk of developing diabetes. Whole grains contain phytochemicals (antioxidants) that improve our body's ability to respond to insulin, which helps us maintain normal blood glucose levels. The fiber found in whole grains also helps to lower blood sugar levels.

Air frying is a healthier way to eat and it helps to maintain under control the level of fat in your balanced diet every day. Most people with diabetes will need to check their blood sugar levels regularly.

Another benefit of air frying is that it helps reduce the risk of developing heart disease and other complications related to diabetes. For example, high blood sugar levels can restrict blood flow to the heart, which can increase the risk of heart attack and stroke. Research shows that ideally a plant-based diet combined with an air fryer can help lower blood sugar levels while improving heart health.

Air fryers are designed to cook food in a minimal quantity of oil at high temperatures; this allows food to be cooked or reheated without adding additional fat, calories, or preservatives. This type of cooking also reduces fat intake and helps people with diabetes follow a healthy diet that greatly health and well-being improves.

What is an Air Fryer

The Air Fryer is an appliance that typically has an egg shape with an internal removable basket where the food is placed to be cooked. The advantage of this appliance is that it uses the concept of air cooking at high temperatures allowing a very healthy fry-not-fry of fresh food. This is because there is no full immersion in the oil. The amount of oil used in the air fryer is a few teaspoons. In the air fryer, the oil never reaches the smoke point and, therefore, is not as toxic as normal frying could be.

The hot air, which reaches high temperatures, circulates in the air fryer chamber allowing the dishes to be cooked evenly both externally and internally. In this way you can cook meat, fish, vegetables and a thousand other dishes in just a few minutes: in short, you can create many recipes. For example, meat cooked in an air fryer can be juicy, very tender and soft.

Excess fats drip to the bottom and do not remain inside the meat, with an exceptional natural flavour.

The hot air is circulated over the surface of the food like it would be in a convection oven. Hot air is circulated around the food from the top and bottom of the frying basket.

How does it work?

Air frying is different from deep-frying or pan-frying because the cooking is done in a very shallow layer of oil and without a pot needed. The hot air circulates cooking the food.

It cooks and gives a crisp texture like deep-fried food, but more evenly cooked inside than in pan-fried foods.

The cooking oils can be olive oil, coconut oil, butter, and no extra flavour is added to the food while they are being cooked for healthier eating options.

It is important always to read and follow the instruction of the specific device for a great result.

The air fryer can cook a whole chicken, fish, or other meat evenly across its surface.

How does an air fryer cook food?

Air fryers use a combination of fans and heat cooking the food. Like any other home oven, they first preheat to a set temperature before you add your food. Then you turn on the convection fan to circulate hot air in all directions; you choose this via the adjustable vent located at the top of most models.

The heated air cooks your food from on each side instead of just one side, as it would be in a traditional pan or on a flat surface like a grill or griddle. As a result, your food will cook much faster and with a more even and crispy texture.

How much do air fryers cost?

Air fryers are not very expensive like some of the other appliances available on the market. They usually come in two varieties: countertop and portable. The countertop air fryers are the larger of the two and tend to be more expensive, but they also offer greater functionality. Portable is a much cheaper option, and you can cook virtually any type of food thanks to their several basket options.

Differences between Type 1 and 2 Diabetes

Type 1 Diabetes

In type 1 diabetes, the pancreas cannot produce insulin due to the destruction of the beta-cells that can produce this hormone. It affects a small percentage of people and typically occurs in childhood or adolescence but can also occur in adults.

Main aspects and facts of type 1:

- it is often diagnosed in childhood;
- is not associated with excess weight;
- it is often associated with a higher than normal level of ketones at the time of diagnosis; let's not forget that the body produces ketones because they are an alternative to the energy source that sugar represents;
- is treated with insulin injections;
- cannot be kept under control without the patient taking insulin;

Type 2 Diabetes

Type 2 diabetes is the most common type and makes up 90% of people with diabetes. This type is called insulin-dependent diabetes, and it is the most prevalent type in adults over 40 years old or overweight. Sometimes it affects children over ten years old and occurs as a result of the body's inability to secrete enough insulin or an adequate amount of the hormone insulin.

Main aspects and facts of type 2:

- it is usually diagnosed in people over the age of 30;
- it is often associated with being overweight;
- is most often associated with high blood pressure and/or high cholesterol at the time of diagnosis;
- usually, it is initially treated without drug treatment or with tablets;
- sometimes it is possible for the patient to get out of the treatment prescribed for diabetes.

The percentage of patients with diabetes that are diagnosed is still not very high because there are few and insufficient symptoms or some similar symptoms to other diseases in the early stages.

If left untreated, the disease can affect vision, heart problems, and kidney failure.

This type requires a regular and balanced diet, sport and medication.

2. Breakfast

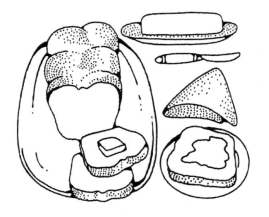

Breakfast

1. <u>Tuna Sandwiches</u>

Preparation Time: 10 minutes **Cooking Time:** 5 minutes

Ingredients   (**Servings:** 2)

- 16 oz. tuna, canned and drained
- ¼ C. mayonnaise
- 2 tbsp. mustard
- 1 tbsp. lemon juice
- 2 green onions, chopped
- 3 English muffins, halved
- 3 tbsp. butter
- 6 provolone cheese

Directions

1. In a bowl, mix tuna with mayo, lemon juice, mustard, and green onions and stir.
2. Grease muffin halves with the butter, place them in the preheated air fryer and bake them at 350ºF for 4 minutes.
3. Spread tuna mix on muffin halves, top each with cheese, return sandwiches to air fryer and cook them for 4 minutes, divide among plates and serve for breakfast right away.

Nutrition

Calories: 182 kcal. **Fat:** 4 g. **Fiber:** 7 g. **Carbs:** 8 g. **Protein:** 6 g.

2. Garlic Potatoes with Bacon

Preparation Time: 10 minutes **Cooking Time:** 20 minutes

Ingredients   (**Servings:** 2)

- 4 potatoes, peeled and cut into medium cubes
- 6 garlic cloves, minced
- 4 bacon slices, chopped
- 2 rosemary springs, chopped
- 1 tbsp. olive oil
- Salt and black pepper to the taste
- 2 eggs, whisked

Directions

1. In the air fryer pan, mix oil with potatoes, garlic, bacon, rosemary, salt, pepper, and eggs and whisk.
2. Cook potatoes at 400ºF for 20 minutes, divide everything between plates and serve for breakfast.

Nutrition

Calories: 211 kcal. **Fat:** 3 g. **Fiber:** 5 g. **Carbs:** 8 g. **Protein:** 5 g.

3. Chicken and Zucchini Omelette

Preparation Time: 15 minutes **Cooking Time:** 35 minutes

Ingredients   (**Servings:** 2)

- 8 eggs
- ½ C. milk
- Salt and black pepper, ground, as required
- 1 C. chicken, cooked and chopped
- 1 C. Cheddar cheese, shredded
- ½ C. fresh chives, chopped
- ¾ C. zucchini, chopped

Directions

1. In a bowl, add the eggs, milk, salt, and black pepper and beat well. Add the remaining ingredients and stir to combine. Place the mixture into a greased baking pan. Press the "Power Button" of Air Fry and turn the dial to select the "Air Bake" mode.

2. Press the Time button and again turn the dial to set the cooking time to 35 minutes. Set the temperature at 315ºF.

3. Press the "Start/Pause" button to start. When the unit beeps to show that it is preheated, open the lid. Arrange pan over the "Wire Rack" and insert in the oven.

4. Cut into equal-sized wedges and serve hot.

Nutrition

Calories: 209 kcal.　**Fat:** 13.3 g.　**Carbs:** 2.3 g.　**Fiber:** 0.3 g.　**Protein:** 9.8 g.

4. Shrimp Frittata

Preparation Time: 10 minutes　**Cooking Time:** 15 minutes

Ingredients　(**Servings:** 2)

- 4 eggs
- ½ tsp. basil, dried
- Cooking spray
- Salt and black pepper to the taste
- ½ C. rice, cooked (optional)
- ½ C. shrimp, cooked, peeled, deveined, and chopped
- ½ C. baby spinach, chopped
- ½ C. Monterey jack cheese, grated

Directions

1. In a bowl, mix eggs with salt, pepper, and basil and whisk. Grease your air fryer's pan with cooking spray and add rice, shrimp, and spinach. Add eggs mix, sprinkle cheese all over and cook in your air fryer at 350ºF for 10 minutes.
2. Divide among plates and serve for breakfast.

Nutrition

Calories: 162 kcal. **Fat:** 6 g. **Fiber:** 5 g. **Carbs:** 8 g. **Protein:** 4 g

5. <u>Chicken Omelette</u>

Preparation Time: 10 minutes **Cooking Time:** 16 minutes

Ingredients (**Servings:** 2)

- 1 tsp. butter
- 1 small yellow onion, chopped
- ½ jalapeño pepper, seeded and chopped
- 3 eggs
- Salt and black pepper, ground, as required
- ¼ C. chicken, cooked and shredded

Directions

1. In a frying pan, melt the butter over medium heat and cook the onion for about 4–5 minutes. Add the jalapeño pepper and cook for about 1 minute.

2. Remove from the heat and set aside to cool slightly. Meanwhile, in a bowl, add the eggs, salt, and black pepper and beat well.

3. Add the onion mixture and chicken and stir to combine. Place the chicken mixture into a small baking pan.

4. Press the Time button and again turn the dial to set the cooking time to 6 minutes.

5. Now push the Temp button and rotate the dial to set the temperature at 355ºF.

6. Press the "Start/Pause" button to start.

7. When the unit beeps to show that it is preheated, open the lid.

8. Arrange pan over the "Wire Rack" and insert in the oven.

9. Cut the omelette into 2 portions and serve hot.

Nutrition

Calories: 153 kcal. **Fat:** 9.1 g. **Carbs:** 4 g. **Fiber:** 0.9 g. **Protein:** 13.8 g.

6. Scrambled Eggs

Preparation Time: 5 minutes   **Cooking Time:** 20 minutes

Ingredients   (**Servings:** 2)

- 4 large eggs
- ½ C. sharp cheese, shredded
- 2 tbsp. unsalted butter

Directions

1. Put eggs into a 2-cup round baking dish and whisk.
2. Place dish into the air fryer basket.
3. Adjust the temperature to 400ºF and set the timer for 10 minutes.
4. After 5 minutes, stir the eggs and add butter and cheese.
5. Let cook for 3 more minutes and stir again.
6. Allow eggs to finish cooking for additional 2 minutes or remove if they are to your desired liking.

Nutrition

Calories: 359 kcal. **Protein:** 19.5 g. **Fat:** 27.6 g. **Carbs:** 1.1g.

7. **Mushroom Cheese Salad**

Preparation Time: 10 minutes **Cooking Time:** 15 minutes

Ingredients   (**Servings:** 2)

- 10 mushrooms, halved
- 1 tbsp. fresh parsley, chopped
- 1 tbsp. olive oil
- 1 tbsp. mozzarella cheese, grated
- 1 tbsp. cheddar cheese, grated
- 1 tbsp. mix herbs, dried
- Pepper
- Salt

Directions

1. Add all ingredients into the bowl and toss well
2. Transfer bowl mixture into the air fryer baking dish
3. Place in the air fryer and cook at 380ºF for 15 minutes.
4. Serve.

Nutrition

Calories: 90 kcal.   **Fat:** 7 g.   **Carbs: 2** g.   **Sugar:** 1 g.   **Protein:** 5 g.

8. Shrimp Sandwiches

Preparation Time: 10 minutes **Cooking Time:** 5 minutes

Ingredients   (**Servings:** 2)

- 1-¼ C. cheddar, shredded
- 6 oz. tiny shrimp, canned and drained
- 3 tbsp. mayonnaise
- 2 tbsp. green onions, chopped
- 4 whole-wheat bread slices
- 2 tbsp. butter, soft

Directions

1. In a bowl, mix shrimp with cheese, green onion, and mayo, and stir well. Spread this on half of the bread slices, top with the other bread slices, cut into halves diagonally, and spread butter on top.
2. Place sandwiches in your air fryer and cook at 350ºF for 5 minutes.
3. Divide shrimp sandwiches between plates and serve them for breakfast.

Nutrition

Calories: 162 kcal. **Fat:** 3 g. **Fiber:** 7 g. **Carbs:** 12 g. **Protein:** 4 g.

9. <u>Mushrooms and Cheese Spread</u>

Preparation Time: 5 minutes   **Cooking Time:** 20 minutes

Ingredients   (**Servings:** 4)

- ¼ C. mozzarella; shredded
- ½ C. coconut cream
- 1 C. white mushrooms
- A pinch salt and black pepper
- Cooking spray

Directions

1. Put the mushrooms in your air fryer's basket, grease with cooking spray, and cook at 370°F for 20 minutes.
2. Transfer to a blender, add the remaining ingredients, blend well, divide into bowls and serve as a spread.

Nutrition

Calories: 202 kcal. **Fat:** 12 g. **Fiber:** 2 g. **Carbs:** 5 g. **Protein:** 7 g.

10.   <u>Lemony Raspberries Bowls</u>

Preparation Time: 5 minutes   **Cooking Time:** 12 minutes

Ingredients   (**Servings:** 2)

- 1 C. raspberries
- 2 tbsp. butter
- 2 tbsp. lemon juice
- 1 tsp. cinnamon powder

Directions

1. In your air fryer, mix all the ingredients, toss, cover, cook at 350°F for 12 minutes, divide into bowls and serve for breakfast.

Nutrition

    Calories: 208 kcal. **Fat:** 6 g. **Fiber:** 9 g. **Carbs:** 14 g. **Protein:** 3 g.

11.   Zucchini Squash Mix

Preparation Time: 10 minutes **Cooking Time:** 35 minutes

Ingredients   (**Servings:** 2)

- 1 lb. zucchini, sliced
- 1 tbsp. parsley, chopped
- 1 yellow squash, halved, deseeded, and chopped
- 1 tbsp. olive oil
- Pepper
- Salt

Directions

1. Add all ingredients into the large bowl and mix well.
2. Transfer the bowl mixture into the air fryer basket and cook at 400ºF for 35 minutes.

Nutrition

    Calories: 49 kcal. **Fat:** 3 g. **Carbs:** 4 g. **Sugar:** 2 g. **Protein:** 1.5 g.

12.   **Onion Omelette**

Preparation Time: 10 minutes **Cooking Time:** 15 minutes

Ingredients   (**Servings:** 2)

- 4 eggs
- ¼ tsp. low-sodium soy sauce
- Black pepper, ground, as required
- 1 tsp. butter
- 1 medium yellow onion, sliced
- ¼ C. Cheddar cheese, grated

Directions

1. In a skillet, melt the butter over medium heat and cook the onion and cook for about 8–10 minutes.
2. Remove from the heat and set aside to cool slightly.
3. Meanwhile, in a bowl, add the eggs, soy sauce, and black pepper and beat well.
4. Add the cooked onion and gently, stir to combine.
5. Set the cooking time to 5 minutes.
6. Set the temperature at 355ºF. Press the "Start/Pause" button to start.
7. When the unit beeps to show that it is preheated, open the lid.
8. Arrange pan over the "Wire Rack" and insert in the oven.
9. Cut the omelette into 2 portions and serve hot.

Nutrition

Calories: 222 kcal.   **Fat:** 15.4 g.   **Fat:** 6.9 g.   **Carbs:** 6.1 g.   **Fiber:** 1.2g.   **Protein:** 15.3 g.

13. Tuna and Spring Onions Salad

Preparation Time: 5 minutes **Cooking Time:** 15 minutes

Ingredients **(Servings:** 4)

- 14 oz. tuna, canned, drained, and flaked
- 2 spring onions, chopped.
- 1 C. arugula
- 1 tbsp. olive oil
- A pinch salt and black pepper

Directions

1. In a bowl, all the ingredients except the oil and the arugula and whisk.

2. Preheat the Air Fryer over 360°F, add the oil and grease it. Pour the tuna mix, stir well, and cook for 15 minutes.

3. In a salad bowl, combine the arugula with the tuna mix, toss and serve.

Nutrition

Calories: 212 kcal. **Fat:** 8 g. **Fiber:** 3 g. **Carbs:** 5 g. **Protein:** 8 g.

14. <u>Breakfast Pea Tortilla</u>

Preparation Time: 10 minutes **Cooking Time:** 7 minutes

Servings: 2 **Ingredients**

- ½ lb. baby peas
- 4 tbsp. butter
- 1 ½ C. yogurt
- 8 eggs
- ½ C. mint, chopped
- Salt and black pepper to the taste

Directions

1. Heat a pan that fits your air fryer with the butter over medium heat, add peas, stir, and cook for a couple of minutes.

2. Meanwhile, in a bowl, mix half of the yogurt with salt, pepper, eggs, and mint and whisk well.

3. Pour this over the peas, toss, introduce in your air fryer and cook at 350ºF for 7 minutes.

4. Spread the rest of the yogurt over your tortilla, slice, and serve.

Nutrition

Calories: 192 kcal. **Fat:** 5 g. **Fiber:** 4 g. **Carbs:** 8 g. **Protein:** 7 g.

15.   Sweet Nuts Butter

Preparation Time: 10 minute **Cooking Time:** 25 Minutes

Ingredients   (Servings: 5)

- 1 ½ lb. sweet potatoes, peeled and cut into ½ inch pieces (2 medium)
- ½ tbsp. olive oil
- 1 tbsp. butter, melted
- 1 tbsp. walnuts, finely chopped
- ½ tsp. one orange, grated
- ⅛ tsp. nutmeg
- ⅛ tsp. cinnamon, ground

Directions

1. Put sweet potatoes in a small bowl and sprinkle with oil. Stir until covered and then pour into the basket, ensuring that they are in a single layer.
2. Cook at a temperature of 350°F for 20 to 25 minutes, stirring or turning halfway through cooking.
3. Remove them to the serving plate.
4. Combine the butter, nuts, orange zest, nutmeg, and cinnamon in a small bowl and pour the mixture over the sweet potatoes.

Nutrition

Calories: 141 kcal. **Fat:** 1.01 g. **Carbohydrates:** 6.68 g. **Protein:** 1.08 g.

3. Vegetables and Sides

Mark Spencer

Vegetables and Sides

16.   <u>Onion Rings</u>

Preparation Time: 10 minutes **Cooking Time:** 20 minutes

Ingredients   (**Servings:** 4)

- 1 large white onion, peeled
- ⅔ C. pork rinds
- 3 tbsp. almond flour
- ½ tsp. garlic powder
- ½ tsp. paprika
- ¼ tsp. sea salt
- 3 tbsp. coconut flour
- 2 eggs, pastured

Directions

1. Switch on the air fryer, insert fryer basket, grease it with olive oil, set the fryer at 400°F, and preheat for 10 minutes.
2. Meanwhile, slice the peeled onion into ½ inch thick rings.
3. Take a shallow dish, add almond flour, and stir in garlic powder, paprika, and pork rinds; take another shallow dish, add coconut flour, and salt and stir until mixed.
4. Crack eggs in a bowl and then whisk until combined.
5. Working on 1 onion ring at a time, first coat onion ring in coconut flour mixture, then it in egg, and coat with pork rind mixture by scooping over the onion until evenly coated.

6. Open the fryer, place coated onion rings in a single layer, spray oil over onion rings, close the lid, and cook for 16 minutes until nicely golden and thoroughly cooked, flipping the onion rings halfway through the frying.

7. When the air fryer beeps, open its lid, transfer onion rings onto a serving plate and cook the remaining onion rings in the same manner.

Nutrition

Calories: 135 kcal. **Fat:** 7 g. **Carbohydrates:** 8 g. **Proteins:** 8 g.

17.   Cauliflower Fritters

Preparation Time: 10 minutes **Cooking Time:** 14 minutes

Ingredients   (**Servings:** 2)

- 5 C. cauliflower florets, chopped
- ½ C. almond flour
- ½ tsp. baking powder
- ½ tsp. black pepper, ground
- ½ tsp. salt
- 2 eggs, pastured

Directions

1. Add chopped cauliflower in a blender or food processor, pulse until minced, and then tip the mixture in a bowl.

2. Add remaining ingredients, stir well and then shape the mixture into ⅓-inch patties, an ice cream scoop of mixture per patty.

3. Switch on the air fryer, insert fryer basket, grease it with olive oil, set the fryer at 390°F, and preheat for 5 minutes.

4. Then open the fryer, add cauliflower patties in a single layer, spray oil over patties, close the lid and cook for 14 minutes at 375°F until nicely golden and cooked, flipping the patties halfway through the frying.

5. Serve straight away with the dip.

Nutrition

Calories: 272 kcal. **Fat:** 0.3 g. **Carbohydrates:** 57 g. **Proteins:** 11 g.

18.   Zucchini Fritters

Preparation Time: 20 minutes **Cooking Time:** 12 minutes

Ingredients   (**Servings:** 4)

- 2 medium zucchinis, ends trimmed
- 3 tbsp. almond flour
- 1 tbsp. salt
- 1 tsp. garlic powder
- ¼ tsp. paprika
- ¼ tsp. black pepper, ground
- ¼ tsp. onion powder
- 1 egg, pastured

Directions

1. Wash and pat dry the zucchini, then cut its ends and grate the zucchini.

2. Place grated zucchini in a colander, sprinkle with salt and let it rest for 10 minutes.

3. Then, wrap zucchini in a kitchen cloth, squeeze moisture from it as much as possible, and place dried zucchini in another bowl.

4. Add remaining ingredients into the zucchini and then stir until mixed.

5. Take the fryer basket, line it with parchment paper, grease it with oil, drop zucchini mixture on it by a spoonful, about 1-inch apart, and then spray well with oil.

6. Switch on the air fryer, insert fryer basket, then shut with its lid, set the fryer at 360°F, and cook the fritter for 12 minutes until nicely golden and cooked, flipping the fritters halfway through the frying.

7. Serve straight away.

Nutrition

Calories: 57 kcal. **Fat:** 1 g. **Carbohydrates:** 8 g. **Proteins:** 3 g.

19.   Kale Chips

Preparation Time: 5 minutes **Cooking Time:** 7 minutes

Ingredients   (**Servings:** 2)

- 1 large bunch kale
- ¾ tsp. red chili powder
- 1 tsp. salt
- ¾ tsp. black pepper, ground

Directions

1. Remove the hard spines from the kale leaves, then cut kale into small pieces and place them in a fryer basket.
2. Spray oil over kale, then sprinkle with salt, chili powder, and black pepper and toss until well mixed.
3. Switch on the air fryer, insert fryer basket, then shut with its lid, set the fryer at 375°F, and cook for 7 minutes until kale is crispy, shaking halfway through the frying.
4. When the air fryer beeps, open its lid, transfer kale chips onto a serving plate and serve.

Nutrition

Calories: 66.2 kcal. **Fat:** 4 g. **Carbohydrates:** 7.3 g. **Proteins:** 2.5 g.

20. <u>Zucchini Fries</u>

Preparation Time: 10 minutes **Cooking Time:** 20 minutes

Ingredients   (**Servings:** 2)

- 2 medium zucchinis
- ½ C. almond flour
- $\frac{1}{8}$ tsp. black pepper, ground
- ½ tsp. garlic powder
- $\frac{1}{8}$ tsp. salt
- 1 tsp. Italian seasoning
- ½ C. parmesan cheese, grated and reduced-fat
- 1 egg, pastured, beaten

Directions

1. Set the fryer at 400°F, grease it with olive oil, and preheat for 10 minutes.
2. Meanwhile, cut each zucchini in half and then cut each zucchini half into 4-inch-long pieces, each about ½-inch thick.
3. Place flour in a shallow dish, add remaining ingredients except for the egg and stir until mixed.
4. Crack the egg in a bowl and then whisk well.
5. Working on one zucchini piece at a time, first dip it in the egg, then coat it in the almond flour mixture and place it on a wire rack.
6. Open the fryer, add zucchini pieces in a single layer, spray oil over zucchini, close the lid and cook for 10 minutes until nicely golden and crispy.

Nutrition

Calories: 147 kcal. **Fat:** 10 g. **Carbohydrates:** 6 g. **Proteins:** 9 g.

21. Avocado Fries

Preparation Time: 10 minutes **Cooking Time:** 20 minutes

Ingredients   (**Servings:** 2)

- 1 medium avocado, pitted
- 1 egg
- ½ C. almond flour
- ¼ tsp. salt
- ¼ tsp. black pepper, ground
- ½ tsp. salt

Directions

1. Switch on the air fryer, insert fryer basket, grease it with olive oil, then shut with its lid, set the fryer at 400°F, and preheat for 10 minutes.
2. Meanwhile, cut the avocado in half and then cut each half into wedges, each about ½-inch thick.
3. Place flour in a shallow dish, add salt and black pepper and stir until mixed.
4. Crack the egg in a bowl and then whisk it until blended.
5. Working on one avocado piece at a time, first dip it in the egg, then coat it in the almond flour mixture and place it on a wire rack.
6. Open the fryer, add avocado pieces in a single layer, spray oil over avocado, close the lid and cook for 10 minutes until nicely golden and crispy.

Nutrition

Calories: 251 kcal. **Fat:** 17 g. **Carbohydrates:** 19 g. **Proteins:** 6 g.

22.　**Roasted Chickpeas**

Preparation Time: 35 minutes　**Cooking Time:** 25 minutes

Ingredients　**(Servings:** 6)

- 15 oz. chickpeas, cooked
- 1 tsp. garlic powder
- 1 tbsp. Nutritional yeast
- ⅛ tsp. cumin
- 1 tsp. paprika, smoked
- ½ tsp. salt
- 1 tbsp. olive oil

Directions

1. Take a large baking sheet, line it with paper towels, spread chickpeas on it, cover the peas with paper towels, and rest for 30 minutes or until chickpeas are dried.
2. Then switch on the air fryer, insert the fryer basket, grease it with olive oil, then shut with its lid, set the fryer at 355°F, and preheat for 5 minutes.
3. Place dried chickpeas in a bowl, add remaining ingredients and toss until well coated.
4. Open the fryer, add chickpeas in it, close the lid and cook for 20 minutes until nicely golden and crispy, shaking the chickpeas every 5 minutes.
5. When the air fryer beeps, open its lid, transfer chickpeas onto a serving bowl, and serve.

Nutrition

Calories: 124 kcal. **Fat:** 4.4 g. **Carbohydrates:** 17.4 g. **Proteins:** 4.7 g.

23.   Buffalo Cauliflower Wings

Preparation Time: 5 minutes **Cooking Time:** 20 minutes

Ingredients   (**Servings:** 6)

- 1 tbsp. almond flour
- 1 medium head cauliflower
- 1 ½ tsp. salt
- 4 tbsp. hot sauce
- 1 tbsp. olive oil

Directions

1. Switch on the air fryer, insert fryer basket, grease it with olive oil, then shut with its lid, set the fryer at 400°F, and preheat for 5 minutes.
2. Meanwhile, cut cauliflower into bite-size florets and set aside.
3. Place flour in a large bowl, whisk in salt, oil, and hot sauce until combined, add cauliflower florets and toss until combined.
4. Open the fryer, add cauliflower florets in a single layer, close the lid and cook for 15 minutes until nicely golden and crispy, shaking halfway through the frying.
5. When the air fryer beeps, open its lid, transfer cauliflower florets onto a serving plate and keep warm.
6. Cook the remaining cauliflower florets in the same manner and serve.

Nutrition

Calories: 48 kcal. **Fat:** 4 g. **Carbohydrates:** 1 g. **Proteins:** 1 g.

24.   __Brussels Sprouts__

Preparation Time: 5 minutes **Cooking Time:** 10 minutes

Ingredients   (Servings: 2)

- 2 C. Brussels sprouts
- ¼ tsp. sea salt
- 1 tbsp. olive oil
- 1 tbsp. apple cider vinegar

Directions

1. Switch on the air fryer, insert fryer basket, grease it with olive oil, then shut with its lid, set the fryer at 400°F, and preheat for 5 minutes.

2. Meanwhile, cut the sprouts lengthwise into ¼-inch thick pieces, add them to a bowl, add remaining ingredients and toss until well coated.

3. Open the fryer, add sprouts to it, close the lid and cook for 10 minutes until crispy and cooked, shaking halfway through the frying.

4. When the air fryer beeps, open its lid, transfer sprouts onto a serving plate, and serve.

Nutrition

Calories: 88 kcal. **Fat:** 4.4 g. **Carbohydrates:** 11 g. **Proteins:** 3.9 g.

25. <u>Green Beans</u>

Preparation Time: 5 minutes **Cooking Time:** 13 minutes

Ingredients   (**Servings:** 4)

- 1-lb. green beans
- ¾ tsp. garlic powder
- ¾ tsp. black pepper, ground
- 1 ¼ tsp. salt
- ½ tsp. paprika

Directions

1. Switch on the air fryer, insert fryer basket, grease it with olive oil, then shut with its lid, set the fryer at 400°F, and preheat for 5 minutes.

2. Meanwhile, place beans in a bowl, spray generously with olive oil, sprinkle with garlic powder, black pepper, salt, and paprika and toss until well coated.

3. Open the fryer, add green beans to it, close the lid and cook for 8 minutes until nicely golden and crispy, shaking halfway through the frying.

4. When the air fryer beeps, open its lid, transfer green beans onto a serving plate and serve.

Nutrition

Calories: 45 kcal. **Fat:** 1 g. **Carbohydrates:** 7 g. **Proteins:** 2 g.

26.   Crunchy Brussels Sprouts

Preparation Time: 9 minutes **Cooking Time:** 5 minutes

Ingredients   **(Servings:** 2)

- 1 tsp. avocado oil
- ½ tsp. black pepper, ground
- ½ tsp. salt
- 10 oz. Brussels sprouts, halved
- ⅓ tsp. balsamic vinegar

Directions

1. Heat the air fryer at 350°F.
2. Mix salt, pepper, and oil together in a bowl. Add the sprouts and toss.
3. Fry the Brussels sprouts in the air fryer for 5 minutes.

Nutrition

Calories: 92 kcal. **Fat:** 3.1 g. **Carbohydrates:** 12.1 g. **Proteins:** 5.2 g.

27.   Buffalo Cauliflower

Preparation Time: 11 minutes **Cooking Time:** 30 minutes

Ingredients   **(Servings:** 4)

- 1 large cauliflower
- 1 C. flour
- ¼ tsp. each
- Chili powder
- Cayenne pepper
- Paprika
- 1 C. soy milk
- 2 tbsp. butter
- 2 garlic cloves, minced
- ½ C. cayenne pepper sauce
- 1 serving cooking spray

Directions

1. Cut the cauliflower into small pieces. Rinse under cold water and drain.

2. Mix the flour, chili powder, cayenne, and paprika in a bowl. Add the milk slowly to make a thick batter.

3. Add the pieces of cauliflower to the batter and coat well.

4. Cook the cauliflower in the air fryer for 20 minutes. Toss the cauliflower and cook again for 10 minutes.

5. Take a saucepan and heat the butter in it. Add garlic and hot sauce. Boil the sauce mixture and simmer for 2 minutes.

6. Transfer the cauliflower to a large bowl and pour the prepared sauce over the cooked cauliflower. Toss for combining.

7. Serve hot.

Nutrition

Calories: 190 kcal. **Fat:** 12 g. **Carbohydrates:** 2.3 g. **Proteins:** 12.3 g.

28. <u>Stuffed Mushrooms</u>

Preparation Time: 12 minutes **Cooking Time:** 10–15 minutes

Ingredients   (**Servings:** 6)

- 15 button mushrooms
- 1 tsp. olive oil
- ⅛ tsp. salt
- ½ tsp. black pepper, crushed
- ⅓ tsp. balsamic vinegar

For the filling:

- ¼ C. each
- Bell pepper
- Onion
- 2 tbsp. cilantro, chopped
- 1 tbsp. jalapeno, chopped finely
- ½ C. mozzarella cheese, grated
- 1 tsp. coriander, ground
- ¼ tsp. each
- Paprika
- Salt

Directions

1. Use a damp cloth for cleaning the mushrooms. Remove the stems to make the caps hollow.
2. Take a bowl and season the mushroom caps with salt, oil, balsamic vinegar, and black pepper.
3. Take another bowl and mix the ingredients for the filling.
4. Use a spoon to fill the mushroom caps. Press the filling in the mushroom using the backside of the spoon.
5. Cook the mushrooms in the air fryer for 10 minutes.

Nutrition

Calories: 42 kcal. **Fat:** 1.2 g. **Carbohydrates:** 2.9 g. **Proteins:** 3.1 g.

29.   Sweet Potatoes With Baked Taquitos

Preparation Time: 5 minutes **Cooking Time:** 20 minutes

Ingredients   (**Servings:** 5)

- 1 sweet potato, cut in ½ inch
- 2 tsp. Canola oil
- ½ C. yellow onion, chopped
- 1 garlic clove, minced
- 2 C. black beans, rinsed
- 1 chipotle pepper, chopped
- ½ tsp. each
- Paprika
- Cumin
- Chili powder
- Maple syrup
- $\frac{1}{8}$ tsp. salt
- 3 tbsp. water
- 10 corn tortillas

Directions

1. Place the pieces of sweet potatoes in an air fryer and toss them with some oil. Cook for 12 minutes. Make sure you shake the basket in between.
2. Take a skillet and heat some oil in it. Add the garlic and onions. Sauté for 5 minutes until the onions are translucent.
3. Add chipotle pepper, beans, paprika, cumin, chili powder, maple syrup, and salt. Add 2 tbsp. water and mix all the ingredients.
4. Add cooked potatoes and mix well.
5. Warm the corn tortillas in a skillet.
6. Put 2 tbsp. beans and potato mixture in a row across the corn tortillas. Grab one end of the corn tortillas and roll them. Tuck the end under the mixture of sweet potato and beans.

7. Place the taquitos with the seam side down in the basket. Spray the taquitos with some oil. Air fry the prepared taquitos for 10 minutes.

8. Serve hot.

Nutrition

Calories: 112 kcal. **Fat:** 1.6 g. **Carbohydrates:** 19.3 g. **Proteins:** 5.2 g.

30.   Cauliflower Curry

Preparation Time: 8 minutes **Cooking Time:** 15 minutes

Ingredients   (Servings: 3)

- 1 C. vegetable stock
- ¾ C. coconut milk (light)
- 2 tsp. Curry powder
- 1 tsp. garlic puree
- ½ tsp. turmeric

- 12 oz. cauliflower, cut in florets
- 1 ½ C. sweet corn kernels
- 3 spring onions, sliced
- Salt

For the topping:

- Lime wedges
- 2 tbsp. cranberries, dried

Directions

1. Heat your air fryer at 374°F.

2. Mix all ingredients in a large bowl and combine well.

3. Transfer the cauliflower mixture to the air fryer basket.

4. Cook for 15 minutes. Give it a mix in the middle.

Nutrition

Calories: 160 kcal. **Proteins:** 5.2 g. **Carbohydrates:** 27.2 g. **Fat:** 3.1 g.

4. Lunch

Lunch

31.   <u>Tilapia</u>

Preparation Time: 5 minutes **Cooking Time:** 12 minutes

Ingredients   (**Servings:** 2)

- 2 tilapia fillets, wild-caught, 1 ½ inch thick
- 1 tsp. old bay seasoning
- ¾ tsp. lemon-pepper seasoning
- ½ tsp. salt

Directions

1. Switch on the Air Fryer, insert fryer basket, grease it with olive oil, then shut with its lid, set the fryer to 400°F, and preheat for 5 minutes.
2. Meanwhile, spray tilapia fillets with oil and then season with salt, lemon, pepper, and old bay seasoning until evenly coated.
3. Open the fryer, add tilapia in it, close the lid and cook for 7 minutes until nicely golden and cooked, turning the fillets halfway through the frying.
4. When the Air Fryer beeps, open its lid, transfer tilapia fillets onto a serving plate and serve.

Nutrition

Calories: 36 kcal. **Carbs:** 0 g. **Fat:** 0.75 g. **Protein:** 7.4 g.

32.   Tomato Basil Scallops

Preparation Time: 5 minutes **Cooking Time:** 15 minutes

Ingredients   **(Servings:** 2)

- 8 jumbo sea scallops, wild-caught
- 1 tbsp. tomato paste
- 12 oz. spinach, frozen, thawed and drained
- 1 tbsp. fresh basil, chopped
- 1 tsp. black pepper, ground
- 1 tsp. garlic, minced
- 1 tsp. salt
- ¾ C. heavy whipping cream, reduced-fat

Directions

1. Greaser the fryer pan, set the fryer to 350°F, and preheat for 5 minutes.
2. Meanwhile, take a 7 inches baking pan, grease it with oil, and place spinach in a single layer.
3. Spray the scallops with oil, sprinkle with ½ tsp. each of salt and black pepper, and then place scallops over the spinach.
4. Place tomato paste in a bowl, whisk in cream, basil, garlic, and remaining salt and black pepper until smooth, and then pour over the scallops.
5. Open the fryer, place the pan in it, close the lid, and cook for 10 minutes until thoroughly cooked and sauce is hot.

Nutrition

Calories: 359 kcal. **Carbs:** 6 g. **Fat:** 33 g. **Protein:** 9 g. **Fiber:** 1 g.

33. **<u>Shrimp Scampi</u>**

Preparation Time: 5 minutes **Cooking Time:** 12 minutes

Ingredients **(Servings:** 4)

- 1-lb. shrimp, peeled, deveined
- 1 tbsp. garlic, minced
- 1 tbsp. basil, minced
- 1 tbsp. lemon juice
- 1 tsp. chives, dried
- 1 tsp. basil, dried
- 2 tsp. red pepper flakes
- 4 tbsp. butter, unsalted
- 2 tbsp. chicken stock

Directions

1. Switch on the Air Fryer, insert fryer pan, grease it with olive oil, then shut with its lid, set the fryer to 330°F, and preheat for 5 minutes.
2. Add butter in it along with red pepper and garlic and cook for 2 minutes or until the butter has melted.
3. Then add remaining ingredients in the pan, stir until mixed and continue cooking for 5 minutes until shrimps have cooked, stirring halfway through.
4. When done, remove the pan from the Air Fryer, stir the shrimp scampi, let it rest for 1 minute and then stir again.
5. Garnish shrimps with basil leaves and serve.

Nutrition

Calories: 221 kcal. **Carbs:** 1 g. **Fat:** 13 g. **Protein:** 23 g. **Fiber:** 0 g.

34. <u>**Salmon Cakes**</u>

Preparation Time: 5 minutes **Cooking Time:** 12 minutes

Ingredients   (**Servings:** 2)

- ½ C. almond flour
- 15 oz. pink salmon, cooked
- ¼ tsp. black pepper, ground
- 2 tsp. Dijon mustard
- 2 tbsp. fresh dill, chopped
- 2 tbsp. mayonnaise, reduced-fat
- 1 egg, pastured
- 2 wedges lemon

Directions

1. Switch on the Air Fryer, insert fryer basket, grease it with olive oil, then shut with its lid, set the fryer to 400°F, and preheat for 5 minutes.

2. Meanwhile, place all the ingredients in a bowl, except for lemon wedges, stir until combined, and then shape into four patties, each about 4-inches.

3. Open the fryer, add salmon patties in it, spray oil over them, close the lid and cook for 12 minutes until nicely golden and crispy, flipping the patties halfway through the frying.

4. When the Air Fryer beeps, open its lid, transfer salmon patties onto a serving plate and serve.

Nutrition

Calories: 517 kcal. **Carbs:** 15 g. **Fat:** 27 g. **Protein:** 52 g. **Fiber:** 5 g.

35.   Tex-Mex Salmon Stir-Fry

Preparation Time: 15 minutes **Cooking Time:** 9 to 14 minutes

Ingredients   (**Servings:** 4)

- 12 oz. salmon fillets, cut into 1½-inch cubes (see Tip)
- 1 red bell pepper, chopped
- 1 red onion, chopped
- 1 jalapeño pepper, minced
- ¼ C. low-sodium salsa
- 2 tbsp. low-sodium tomato juice
- 2 tsp. peanut oil or safflower oil
- 1 tsp. chili powder
- Brown rice or polenta, cooked (optional)

Directions

1. In an intermediate bowl, blend the salmon, red bell pepper, red onion, jalapeño, salsa, tomato juice, peanut oil, and chili powder.

2. Place the bowl in the Air Fryer and cook for 9–14 -minutes, until the salmon is just cooked through and firm and the vegetables are crisp-tender, stirring once. Serve instantly over hot cooked brown rice or polenta, if desired.

Nutrition

Calories: 116 kcal. **Fat:** 3 g. **Protein:** 18 g. **Carbohydrates:** 5 g. **Sodium:** 136 mg.

36.   Scallops With Green Vegetables

Preparation Time: 15 Minutes **Cooking Time:** 8–11 Minutes

Ingredients   **(Servings:** 4)

- 1 C. green beans
- 1 C. peas, frozen
- 1 C. broccoli, frozen and chopped
- 2 tsp. olive oil
- ½ tsp. basil, dried
- ½ tsp. oregano, dried
- 12 oz. sea scallops

Directions

1. In a big bowl, toss the green beans, peas, and broccoli with olive oil. Place in the Air Fryer basket. Air-fry for 4–6 minutes, or until the vegetables are crisp-tender.
2. Remove the vegetables from the Air Fryer basket and sprinkle them with the herbs. Set aside.
3. In the Air Fryer basket, put the scallops and air-fry for 4–5 minutes, or until the scallops are firm and reach an internal temperature of just 145°F on a meat thermometer.
4. Toss scallops with the vegetables and serve immediately.

Nutrition

Calories: 124 kcal **Protein:** 14 g. **Carbohydrates:** 11 g. **Sodium:** 56 mg. **Fiber:** 3 g.

37.   **Cilantro Lime Shrimps**

Preparation Time: 25 minutes **Cooking Time:** 21 minutes

Ingredients   (**Servings:** 4)

- ½-lb. shrimp, peeled, deveined
- ½ tsp. garlic, minced
- 1 tbsp. cilantro, chopped
- ½ tsp. paprika
- ¾ tsp. salt
- ½ tsp. cumin, ground
- 2 tbsp. lemon juice

Directions

1. Switch on the Air Fryer, insert the fryer basket, grease it with olive oil, then shut with its lid, set the fryer at 350ºF, and let preheat.
2. Whisk together lemon juice, paprika, salt, cumin, and garlic in a large bowl, then add shrimps and toss until well coated.
3. Drain the skewers and then thread shrimps in them.
4. Open the fryer, add shrimps in a single layer, spray oil over them, close the lid and cook for 8 minutes until nicely golden and cooked, turning the skewers halfway through the frying.
5. When the Air Fryer beeps, open its lid, transfer shrimps onto a serving plate, and keep them warm.
6. Cook remaining shrimp skewers the same way and serve.

Nutrition

Calories: 59 kcal.. **Carbs:** 0.3 g. **Fat:** 1.5 g. **Protein:** 11 g.

38.   Chicken in Tomato Juice

Preparation Time: 20 minutes **Cooking Time:** 15 minutes

Ingredients   (**Servings:** 3)

- 350 g. chicken fillet
- 200 g. tomato juice
- 100 g. tomatoes
- 2 tsp. basil
- 1 tsp. chili
- 1 tsp. oregano
- 1 tsp. rosemary
- 1 tsp. olive oil
- 1 tsp. mint
- 1 tsp. lemon juice

Directions

1. Take a bowl and make the tomato sauce: combine basil, chili, oregano, rosemary, and olive oil, mint, and lemon juice and stir the mixture very carefully.

2. You can use a hand mixer to mix the mass. It will make the mixture smooth.

3. Take a chicken fillet and separate it into 3 pieces.

4. Put the meat into the tomato mixture and leave for 15 minutes.

5. Meanwhile, preheat the Air Fryer oven to 446 ºF.

6. Put the meat mixture on the tray and put it in the oven for at least 15 minutes.

Nutrition

Calories: 258 kcal. **Proteins:** 34.8 g. **Fats:** 10.5 g. **Carbohydrates:** 5.0 g.

39. Salmon on Bed of Fennel and Carrot

Preparation Time: 15 minutes **Cooking Time:** 13–14 minutes

Ingredients **(Servings:** 2)

- 1 fennel bulb, thinly sliced
- 1 large carrot, peeled and sliced
- 1 small onion, thinly sliced
- ¼ C. low-fat sour cream
- ¼ tsp. coarsely ground pepper
- 2 (5 oz.) salmon fillets

Directions

1. Combine the fennel, carrot, and onion in a bowl and toss.
2. Put the vegetable mixture into a 6-inch metal pan. Roast in the Air Fryer for 4 minutes or until the vegetables are crisp-tender.
3. Remove the pan from the Air Fryer. Stir in the sour cream and sprinkle the vegetables with the pepper.
4. Top with the salmon fillets.
5. Return the pan to the Air Fryer. Roast for another 9–10 minutes or until the salmon just barely flakes when tested with a fork.

Nutrition

Calories: 253 kcal. **Fat:** 9 g. **Protein:** 31 g. **Carbohydrates:** 12 g. **Sodium:** 115 mg. **Fiber:** 3 g.

40. Roasted Vegetable Chicken Salad

Preparation Time: 10 minutes **Cooking Time:** 10–13 minutes

Ingredients   (**Servings:** 4)

- 3 (4-oz.) low-sodium chicken breasts, boneless skinless, cut into 1-inch cubes (see Tip)
- 1 small red onion, sliced
- 1 red bell pepper, sliced
- 1 C. green beans, cut into 1-inch pieces
- 2 tbsp. low-fat ranch salad dressing
- 2 tbsp. lemon juice, freshly squeezed
- ½ tsp. basil, dried
- 4 C. lettuce, mixed

Directions

1. In the Air Fryer basket, roast the chicken, red onion, red bell pepper, and green beans for 10–13 minutes, or until the chicken reaches an internal temperature of 165°F on a meat thermometer, tossing the food in the basket once during cooking.
2. While the chicken cooks, in a serving bowl, mix the ranch dressing, lemon juice, and basil.
3. Transfer the chicken and vegetables to a serving bowl and toss with the dressing to coat. Serve immediately on lettuce leaves.

Nutrition

Calories: 113 kcal.   **Fat:** 1 g. **Protein:** 19 g.

41. Spicy Chicken Meatballs

Preparation Time: 10 minutes **Cooking Time:** 11–14 minutes

Ingredients (**Servings:** 24)

- 1 medium red onion, minced
- 2 garlic cloves, minced
- 1 jalapeño pepper, minced
- 2 tsp. olive oil
- 3 tbsp. ground almonds
- 1 egg
- 1 tsp. thyme, dried
- 1 lb. chicken breast, ground

Directions

1. In a 6-by-2-inch pan, combine the red onion, garlic, jalapeño, and olive oil. Bake for 3–4 minutes in the Air Fryer, or until the vegetables are crisp-tender. Transfer to a medium bowl.

2. Mix in the almonds, egg, and thyme to the vegetable mixture. Add the chicken and mix until just combined.

3. Form the chicken mixture into about 24 (1-inch) balls. Bake the meatballs, in batches, for 8–10 minutes, until the chicken reaches an internal temperature of 165°F on a meat thermometer.

Nutrition

Calories: 185 kcal **Protein:** 29 g. **Carbohydrates:** 5 g. **Sodium:** 55 mg. **Fiber:** 1 g.

42. <u>Chicken Wings With Curry</u>

Preparation Time: 15 minutes **Cooking Time:** 20 minutes

Ingredients   (**Servings:** 4)

- 400 g. chicken wings
- 30 g. curry
- 1 tsp. chili
- 1 tsp. cayenne pepper
- 1 tsp. salt
- 1 lemon
- 1 tsp. basil
- 1 tsp. oregano
- 3 tsp. mustard
- 1 tsp. olive oil

Directions

1. Rub the wings with chili, curry, cayenne pepper, salt, basil, and oregano.
2. Put it in the bowl and mix it very carefully.
3. Leave the mixture at least for 10 minutes in the fridge.
4. Remove the mixture from the fridge and add mustard and sprinkle with chopped lemon. Stir the mixture gently again.
5. Spray the pan with olive oil and put the wings in it.
6. Preheat the Air Fryer oven to 356 ºF and put wings there.
7. Cook it for 20 minutes.

Nutrition

Calories: 244 kcal. **Proteins:** 30.8 g. **Fats:** 10.6 g. **Carbohydrates:** 7.2 g.

43.   Stuffed Chicken

Preparation Time: 15 minutes **Cooking Time:** 30 minutes

Ingredients   (**Servings:** 4)

- 2 chicken breasts
- 2 tomatoes
- 200 g. basil
- 1 tsp. black pepper
- 1 tsp. cayenne pepper
- 100 g. tomato juice
- 40 g. goat cheese

Directions

1. Make a "Pocket" from the chicken breasts and rub it with black pepper and cayenne pepper.

2. Slice tomatoes and chop basil.

3. Chop the goat cheese.

4. Combine all the ingredients together, it will be the filling for breasts.

5. Fill the chicken breasts with this mixture.

6. Take a needle, thread, and sew "Pockets."

7. Preheat the Air Fryer oven to 392 ºF. Place the chicken breasts in the tray and pour it with tomato juice.

8. Serve.

Nutrition

Calories: 312 kcal. **Proteins:** 41.6 g. **Fats:** 13.4 g. **Carbohydrates:** 5.6 g.

44.   __Pork Spare Ribs__

Preparation Time: 15 minutes **Cooking Time:** 20 minutes

Ingredients   (**Servings:** 6)

- 5–6 garlic cloves, minced
- ½ C. rice vinegar
- 2 tbsp. soy sauce
- Salt and black pepper, ground, as required
- 1-inch pork spare ribs
- ½ C. corn-starch
- 2 tbsp. olive oil

Directions

1. In a big bowl, mix the garlic, vinegar, soy sauce, salt, and black pepper.
2. Add the ribs and generously coat with the mixture.
3. Refrigerate to marinate overnight.
4. In a shallow bowl, place the corn-starch.
5. Coat the ribs evenly with corn-starch and then, drizzle with oil.
6. Set the temperature of the Air Fryer to 390ºF. Grease an Air Fryer basket.
7. Arrange ribs into the prepared Air Fryer basket in a single layer.
8. Air fry for about 10 minutes per side.
9. Remove from Air Fryer and transfer the ribs onto serving plates.
10. Serve immediately.

Nutrition

Calories: 557 kcal. **Carbohydrate:** 11 g. **Protein:** 35 g. **Sodium:** 997 mg.

45.   BBQ Pork Ribs

Preparation Time: 15 minutes **Cooking Time:** 26 minutes

Ingredients   **(Servings:** 4)

- ¼ C. honey, divided
- ¾ C. BBQ sauce
- 2 tbsp. tomato ketchup
- 1 tbsp. Worcestershire sauce®
- 1 tbsp. soy sauce
- ½ tsp. garlic powder
- White pepper, freshly ground to taste
- 1 ¾ lb. pork ribs

Directions

1. In a bowl, mix 3 tbsp. honey and the other ingredients except for pork ribs.
2. Add the pork ribs and generously coat with the mixture.
3. Refrigerate to marinate for about 20 minutes.
4. Grease the Air Fryer basket. Set the temperature of the Air Fryer to 355ºF.
5. Arrange ribs into the prepared Air Fryer basket in a single layer.
6. Air fry for about 13 minutes per side.
7. Remove from Air Fryer and transfer the ribs onto plates.
8. Drizzle with the remaining honey and serve immediately.

Nutrition

Calories: 691 kcal.   **Carbohydrates:** 37.7 g. **Protein:** 53.1 g. **Fat:** 31.3 g.
Sodium: 991 mg.

5. Fish and Seafood

Fish and Seafood

46.   Salmon Cakes in Air Fryer

Preparation Time: 10 minute **Cooking Time:** 10 minutes

Ingredients   (**Servings:** 2)

- 8 oz. fresh salmon fillet
- 1 egg
- ⅛ tsp. salt
- ¼ tsp. garlic powder
- 1 lemon, sliced

Directions

1. In the bowl, chop the salmon, add the egg and spices.

2. Form tiny cakes.

3. Let the Air fryer preheat to 390ºF. On the bottom of the air fryer bowl lay sliced lemons, place cakes on top.

4. Cook them for 7 minutes. Based on your diet preferences, eat with your chosen dip.

Nutrition

Calories: 194 kcal. **Fat:** 9 g. **Carbs:** 1 g. **Protein:** 25 g.

47.   Crispy Fish Sticks in Air Fryer

Preparation Time: 10 minutes **Cooking Time:** 15 minutes

Ingredients   (**Servings:** 4)

- 1 lb. whitefish such as cod
- ¼ C. mayonnaise
- 2 tbsp. Dijon mustard
- 2 tbsp. water
- 1 ½ C. pork rind
- ¾ tsp. Cajun seasoning
- Kosher salt and pepper to taste

Directions

1. Spray non-stick cooking spray to the air fryer rack.
2. Pat the fish dry and cut into sticks about 1 inch by 2 inches broad.
3. Stir together the mayo, mustard, and water in a small dish. Mix the pork rinds and Cajun seasoning into another small container.
4. Adding kosher salt and pepper to taste (both pork rinds and seasoning can have a decent amount of kosher salt, so you can dip a finger to see how salty it is).
5. Working for one slice of fish at a time, dip to cover in the mayo mix, and then tap off the excess. Dip into the mixture of pork rind, then flip to cover. Place on the rack of an air fryer.
6. Set at 400ºF to Air Fry and bake for 5 minutes, then turn the fish with tongs and bake for another 5 minutes. Serve.

Nutrition

Calories: 263 kcal. **Fat:** 16 g. **Net Carbs:** 1 g. **Protein:** 26.4 g.

48.   Basil-Parmesan Crusted Salmon

Preparation Time: 5 minutes **Cooking Time:** 15 minutes

Ingredients   (**Servings:** 4)

- 3 tbsp. parmesan, grated
- 4 salmon fillets, skinless
- ¼ tsp. salt
- Black pepper, freshly ground
- 3 tbsp. low-fat mayonnaise
- Basil leaves, chopped
- ½ lemon

Directions

1. Let the air fryer preheat to 400ºF. Spray the basket with olive oil.
2. With salt, pepper, and lemon juice, season the salmon.
3. In a bowl, mix 2 tbsp. Parmesan cheese with mayonnaise and basil leaves.
4. Add this mix and more parmesan on top of salmon and cook for 7 minutes or until fully cooked.
5. Serve hot.

Nutrition

Calories: 289 kcal. **Carbohydrates:** 1.5 g. **Protein:** 30 g. **Fat:** 18.5 g.

49.   <u>Cajun Shrimp in Air Fryer</u>

Preparation Time: 10 minutes **Cooking Time:** 20 minutes

Ingredients   (Servings: 4)

- 24 extra-jumbo shrimp, peeled
- 2 tbsp. olive oil
- 1 tbsp. cajun seasoning
- 1 zucchini, thick slices (half-moons)
- ¼ C. turkey, cooked
- Yellow squash, sliced (half-moons)
- ¼ tsp. Kosher salt

Directions

1. In a bowl, mix the shrimp with Cajun seasoning.
2. In another bowl, add zucchini, turkey, salt, squash, and coat with oil.
3. Let the air fryer preheat to 400ºF.
4. Move the shrimp and vegetable mix to the fryer basket and cook for 3 minutes.
5. Serve hot.

Nutrition

Calories: 284 kcal. **Carbohydrates:** 8 g. **Protein:** 3 g. **Fat:** 14 g.

50.   Air Fryer Fish and Chips

Preparation Time: 10 minutes **Cooking Time:** 35 minutes

Ingredients   (**Servings:** 4)

- 4 C. any fish fillet
- ¼ C. flour
- 1 C. whole-wheat breadcrumbs
- 1 egg
- 2 tbsp. oil
- 2 russet Potatoes
- 1 tsp. salt

Directions

1. Cut the potatoes in fries. Then coat with oil and salt.
2. Cook in the air fryer for 20 minutes at 400ºF, toss the fries halfway through.
3. In the meantime, coat fish in flour, then in the whisked egg, and finally in breadcrumbs mix.
4. Place the fish in the air fryer and let it cook at 330ºF for 15 minutes.
5. Flip it halfway through, if needed.
6. Serve with tartar sauce and salad green.

Nutrition

Calories: 409 kcal. **Carbohydrates:** 44 g. **Protein:** 30 g. **Fat:** 11 g.

51.   <u>Grilled Salmon With Lemon</u>

Preparation Time: 10 minutes   **Cooking Time:** 20 minutes

Ingredients   (**Servings:** 4)

- 2 tbsp. olive oil
- 2 salmon fillets
- Lemon juice
- ⅓ C. water
- ⅓ C. gluten-free light soy sauce
- ⅓ C. honey
- 3 Scallion slices
- Black pepper, freshly ground, garlic powder, and kosher salt to taste

Directions

1. Season salmon with pepper and salt.
2. In a bowl, mix honey, soy sauce, lemon juice, water, oil. Add salmon to this marinade and let it rest for at least 2 hours.
3. Let the air fryer preheat at 356°F.
4. Place fish in the air fryer and cook for 8 minutes.
5. Move to a dish and top with scallion slices.

Nutrition

Calories: 211 kcal. **Fat:** 9 g. **Protein:** 15 g. **Carbs:** 4.9 g.

52.   <u>Garlic Rosemary Grilled Prawns</u>

Preparation Time: 5 minutes **Cooking Time:** 10 minutes

Ingredients   (Servings: 2)

- ½ tbsp. butter, melted
- 2 green capsicum slices
- 8 prawns
- 2 Rosemary leaves
- Kosher salt and black pepper, freshly ground
- 3- 4 garlic cloves, minced

Directions

1. In a bowl, mix all the ingredients and marinate the prawns in it for at least 60 minutes or more
2. Add 2 prawns and 2 slices of capsicum on each skewer.
3. Let the air fryer preheat to 356ºF.
4. Cook for 5–6 minutes. Then change the temperature to 392ºF and cook for another minute.
5. Serve with lemon wedges.

Nutrition

Calories: 194 kcal. **Fat:** 10 g. **Carbohydrates:** 12 g. **Protein:** 26 g.

53.   <u>Air-Fried Crumbed Fish</u>

Preparation Time: 10 minutes **Cooking Time:** 12 minutes

Ingredients   (Servings: 2)

- 4 fish fillets
- 4 tbsp. Olive oil
- 1 egg, beaten
- ¼ C. whole wheat breadcrumbs

Directions

1. Let the air fryer preheat to 356ºF.
2. In a bowl, mix breadcrumbs with oil and mix well.
3. First, coat the fish in the egg mix (egg mix with water), then in the breadcrumb mix and coat well.
4. Place in the air fryer, let it cook for 10–12 minutes.
5. Serve hot with salad green and lemon.

Nutrition

Calories: 254 kcal. **Fat:** 12.7 g. **Carbohydrates:** 10.2 g. **Protein:** 15.5 g.

54.   Parmesan Garlic Crusted Salmon

Preparation Time: 5 minutes **Cooking Time:** 15 minutes

Ingredients   (Servings: 2)

- ¼ C. whole wheat breadcrumbs
- 4 C. salmon
- 2 tbsp. butter melted
- ¼ tsp. black pepper, freshly ground
- ¼ C. parmesan cheese, grated
- 2 tsp. garlic, minced
- ½ tsp. Italian seasoning

Directions

1. Let the air fryer preheat to 400ºF, spray the oil over the air fryer basket.
2. Pat dry the salmon. In a bowl, mix cheese, seasoning, and breadcrumbs. In another pan, mix melted butter with garlic and add to the breadcrumbs mix, continuing mixing well.
3. Add kosher salt and freshly ground black pepper to salmon. On top of every salmon piece, add the crust mix and press gently.
4. Let the air fryer preheat to 400ºF and add salmon to it. Cook until done to your liking.
5. Serve hot with vegetable side dishes.

Nutrition

Calories: 330 kcal. **Fat:** 19 g. **Carbohydrates:** 11 g. **Protein:** 31 g.

55. Air Fryer Salmon With Maple Soy Glaze

Preparation Time: 5 minutes **Cooking Time:** 8 minutes

Ingredients   (**Servings:** 4)

- 3 tbsp. pure maple syrup
- 3 tbsp. gluten-free soy sauce
- 1 tbsp. sriracha hot sauce
- 1 garlic clove, minced
- 4 salmon fillets, skinless

Directions

1. In a bowl, maple syrup, garlic, and soy sauce with salmon.
2. Mix well and let it marinate for at least half an hour.
3. Let the air fryer preheat to 400ºF with oil spray the basket.
4. Take fish out from the marinade, pat dry.
5. Put the salmon in the air fryer, cook for 7–8 minutes, or longer.
6. In the meantime, in a saucepan, add the marinade, let it simmer until reduced to half.
7. Add glaze over salmon and serve.

Nutrition

Calories: 292 kcal. **Carbohydrates:** 12 g. **Protein:** 35 g. **Fat:** 11 g.

56.   <u>Air Fryer Shrimp Scampi</u>

Preparation Time: 5 minutes **Cooking Time:** 10 minutes

Ingredients   (**Servings:** 2)

- 4 C. raw shrimp
- 1 tbsp. lemon juice
- Fresh basil, chopped
- 2 tsp. red pepper flakes
- 2.5 tbsp. butter
- Chives, chopped
- 2 tbsp. chicken stock
- 1 tbsp. garlic, minced

Directions

1. Let the air fryer preheat with a metal pan to 330ºF.
2. In the hot pan, add garlic, red pepper flakes, and half of the butter. Let it cook for 2 minutes.
3. Add the butter, shrimp, chicken stock, minced garlic, chives, lemon juice, basil to the pan. Let it cook for 5 minutes. Bathe the shrimp in melted butter.
4. Take out from the air fryer and let it rest for 1 minute.
5. Add fresh basil leaves and chives and serve.

Nutrition

Calories: 287 kcal. **Fat:** 5.5 g. **Carbohydrates:** 7.5 g. **Protein:** 18 g.

57. Lemon Pepper Shrimp in Air Fryer

Preparation Time: 5 minutes **Cooking Time:** 10 minutes

Ingredients (**Servings:** 2)

- 1-½ C. raw shrimp, peeled, deveined
- ½ tbsp. olive oil
- ¼ tsp. garlic powder
- 1 tsp. lemon pepper
- ¼ tsp. paprika
- 1 lemon, juiced

Directions

1. Let the air fryer preheat to 400ºF.
2. In a bowl, mix lemon pepper, olive oil, paprika, garlic powder, and lemon juice. Mix well and add shrimps and coat well.
3. Add shrimps in the air fryer, cook for 6–8 minutes, and top with lemon slices and serve.

Nutrition

Calories: 237 kcal. **Fat:** 6 g. **Carbohydrates:** 11 g. **Protein:** 36 g.

58.   Lemon Garlic Shrimp in Air Fryer

Preparation Time: 5 minutes **Cooking Time:** 10 minutes

Ingredients   (**Servings:** 2)

- 1 tbsp. olive oil
- 4 C. small shrimp, peeled, tails removed
- 1 lemon juice and zest
- ¼ C. parsley, sliced
- 1 pinch red pepper flakes, crushed
- 4 garlic cloves, grated
- ¼ tsp. sea salt

Directions

1. Let air fryer heat to 400ºF.
2. Mix olive oil, lemon zest, red pepper flakes, shrimp, kosher salt, and garlic in a bowl and coat the shrimp well.
3. Place shrimps in the air fryer basket, coat with oil spray.
4. Cook at 400ºF for 8 minutes. Toss the shrimp halfway through.
5. Serve with lemon slices and parsley.

Nutrition

Calories: 140 kcal. **Fat:** 18 g. **Net Carbs:** 8 g. **Protein:** 20 g.

59.   <u>Juicy Air Fryer Salmon</u>

Preparation Time: 5 minutes **Cooking Time:** 12 minutes

Ingredients   (**Servings:** 4)

- 2 tsp. lemon-pepper seasoning
- 4 C. salmon
- 1 tbsp. olive oil
- 2 tsp. seafood seasoning
- ½ lemon's juice
- 1 tsp. garlic powder:
- Kosher salt to taste

Directions

1. In a bowl, add 1 tbsp. olive oil, and ½ lemon juice.
2. Pour this mixture over salmon and rub. Leave the skin on salmon. It will come off when cooked.
3. Rub the salmon with kosher salt and spices.
4. Put parchment paper in the air fryer basket. Put the salmon in the air fryer.
5. Cook at 360ºF for 10 minutes.
6. Let the salmon rest 5 minutes before serving.
7. Serve with salad greens and lemon wedges.

Nutrition

Calories: 132 kcal. **Fat:** 7.4 g. **Carbohydrates:** 12 g. **Protein:** 22.1 g.

60.　**<u>Crispy Fish Sandwiches</u>**

Preparation Time: 10 minutes　**Cooking Time:** 10 minutes

Ingredients　**(Servings:** 2)

- 2 Cod fillets
- 2 tbsp. all-purpose flour
- ¼ tsp. pepper
- 1 tbsp. lemon juice
- ¼ tsp. salt

- ½ tsp. garlic powder
- 1 egg
- ½ tbsp. mayo
- ½ C. whole wheat bread crumbs

Directions

1. In a bowl, add salt, flour, pepper, and garlic powder.
2. In a separate bowl, add lemon juice, mayo, and egg.
3. In another bowl, add the breadcrumbs.
4. Coat the fish in flour, then in egg, then in breadcrumbs.
5. With cooking oil, spray the basket and put the fish in the basket. Also, spray the fish with cooking oil.
6. Cook at 400ºF for 10 minutes. This fish is soft, be careful when you flip it.

Nutrition

Calories: 218 kcal. **Net Carbs:** 7 g. **Fat:** 12 g. **Protein:** 22 g.

6. Poultry, Pork, and Beef

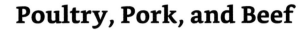

Poultry, Pork, and Beef

61.　Chicken Wings

Preparation Time: 10 minutes **Cooking Time:** 1 hour and 30 minutes

Ingredients　(**Servings:** 4)

- 3 lb. chicken wing parts, pastured
- 1 tbsp. old bay seasoning
- 1 tsp. lemon zest
- ¾ C. potato starch
- ½ C. butter, unsalted, melted

Directions

1. Switch on the air fryer, insert the fryer basket, grease it with olive oil, then shut with its lid, set the fryer at 360ºF, and preheat for 5 minutes.
2. Meanwhile, pat dry chicken wings and then place them in a bowl.
3. Stir together seasoning and starch, add to chicken wings, and stir well until evenly coated.
4. Open the fryer, add the chicken wings in a single layer, close the lid and cook for 35 minutes, flip it every 10 minutes.
5. Then switch the temperature of the air fryer to 400ºF, then continue air frying the chicken wings for 10 minutes or until nicely golden brown and cooked, shaking every 3 minutes.
6. When the air fryer beeps, open its lid, transfer chicken wings onto a serving plate, and cook the remaining wings in the same manner.

7. Whisk together melted butter and lemon zest until blended and serve it with the chicken wings.

Nutrition

Calories: 240 kcal. **Carbs:** 4 g. **Fat:** 16 g. **Protein:** 20 g.

62. <u>**Chicken Nuggets**</u>

Preparation Time: 10 minutes **Cooking Time:** 24 minutes

Ingredients (**Servings:** 4)

- 1-lb. chicken breast, pastured
- ¼ C. coconut flour
- 6 tbsp. sesame seeds, toasted
- ½ tsp. ginger powder
- ⅛ tsp. sea salt
- 1 tsp. sesame oil
- 4 egg whites, pastured

Directions

1. Set the air fryer at 400ºF, and preheat for 10 minutes.
2. Meanwhile, cut the chicken breast into 1-inch pieces, pat them dry, place the chicken pieces in a bowl, sprinkle with salt and oil, and toss until well coated.
3. Place flour in a large plastic bag, add ginger and chicken, seal the bag and turn it upside down to coat the chicken with flour evenly.
4. Place egg whites in a bowl, whisk well, then add coated chicken and toss until well coated.

5. Place sesame seeds in a large plastic bag, add chicken pieces in it, seal the bag and turn it upside down to coat the chicken with sesame seeds evenly.

6. Open the fryer, add chicken nuggets in a single layer, spray with oil, close the lid and cook for 12 minutes until nicely golden and cooked, turning the chicken nuggets and spraying with oil halfway through.

7. When the air fryer beeps, open its lid, transfer the chicken nuggets onto a serving plate and fry the remaining chicken nuggets in the same manner.

8. Serve straight away.

Nutrition

Calories: 312 kcal. **Carbs:** 9 g. **Fat:** 15 g. **Protein:** 33.6 g. **Fiber:** 5 g.

63.   <u>**Chicken Meatballs**</u>

Preparation Time: 5 minutes **Cooking Time:** 26 minutes

Ingredients   (**Servings:** 4)

- 1-lb. chicken, ground
- 2 green onions, chopped
- ¾ tsp. black pepper, ground
- ¼ C. coconut, shredded and unsweetened
- 1 tsp. salt
- 1 tbsp. hoisin sauce
- 1 tbsp. soy sauce
- ½ C. cilantro, chopped
- 1 tsp. Sriracha sauce
- 1 tsp. sesame oil

Directions

1. Switch on the air fryer, insert the fryer basket, grease it with olive oil, then shut with its lid, set the fryer at 350ºF, and preheat for 5 minutes.

2. Meanwhile, place all the ingredients in a bowl, stir until well mixed and then shape the mixture into meatballs, 1 tsp. chicken mixture per meatball.

3. Open the fryer, add chicken meatballs in a single layer, close the lid and then spray with oil.

4. Cook the chicken meatballs for 10 minutes, flipping the meatballs halfway through, and then continue cooking for 3 minutes until golden.

5. When the air fryer beeps, open its lid, transfer the chicken meatballs onto a serving plate and then cook the remaining meatballs in the same manner.

6. Serve straight away.

Nutrition

Calories: 223 kcal. **Carbs:** 3 g. **Fat:** 14 g. **Protein:** 20 g. **Fiber:** 1 g.

64.   <u>**Buffalo Chicken Hot Wings**</u>

Preparation Time: 10 minutes **Cooking Time:** 45 minutes

Ingredients   (**Servings:** 6)

- 16 chicken wings, pastured
- 1 tsp. garlic powder
- 2 tsp. chicken seasoning
- ¾ tsp. black pepper, ground
- 2 tsp. soy sauce
- ¼ C. buffalo sauce, reduced-fat

Directions

1. Switch on the air fryer, insert the fryer basket, grease it with olive oil, then shut with its lid, set the fryer at 400ºF, and preheat for 5 minutes.

2. Meanwhile, place chicken wings in a bowl, drizzle with soy sauce, toss until well coated, and then season with black pepper and garlic powder.

3. Open the fryer, stack chicken wings in it, then spray with oil and close the lid.

4. Cook the chicken wings for 10 minutes, turning the wings halfway through, and then transfer them to a bowl, covering the bowl with a foil to keep the chicken wings warm.

5. Air fry the remaining chicken wings in the same manner, then transfer them to the bowl, add buffalo sauce and toss until well coated.

6. Return chicken wings into the fryer basket in a single layer and continue frying for 7–12 minutes or until chicken wings are glazed and crispy, shaking the chicken wings every 3–4 minutes.

7. Serve straight away.

Nutrition

    Calories: 88 kcal. **Carbs:** 2.6 g. **Fat:** 6.5 g. **Protein:** 4.5 g. **Fiber:** 0.1 g.

65. <u>Lemon Pepper Chicken</u>

Preparation Time: 1 hour and 10 minutes **Cooking Time:** 28 minutes

Ingredients   (**Servings:** 4)

- 4 chicken breasts, pastured
- ¼ C. lemon juice
- 2 tsp. Worcestershire sauce
- ¼ C. olive oil

Directions

1. Prepare the marinade, and for this, place oil, Worcestershire sauce, salt, and lemon juice in a bowl and whisk until combined.

2. Cut each chicken breast into four pieces, add the chicken pieces into the marinade, toss until well coated, and marinate the chicken in the refrigerator for a minimum of 1 hour.

3. Then switch on the air fryer, insert the fryer basket, grease it with olive oil, then shut with its lid, set the fryer at 350ºF, and preheat for 5 minutes.

4. Open the fryer, add chicken pieces in a single layer, spray with oil, close the lid and cook for 14 minutes at 350ºF until nicely golden and cooked, turning the chicken halfway through the frying.

5. When the air fryer beeps, open its lid, transfer the chicken onto a serving plate and cook the remaining chicken pieces in the same manner.

Nutrition

Calories: 55 kcal. **Carbs:** 1.3 g. **Fat:** 2.7 g. **Protein:** 6.6 g. **Fiber:** 0.5 g.

66.   <u>**Pork Burgers With Red Cabbage Slaw**</u>

Preparation Time: 20 minutes **Cooking Time:** 7–9 minutes

Ingredients   (Servings: 4)

- ½ C. Greek yogurt
- 2 tbsp. low-sodium mustard, divided
- 1 tbsp. lemon juice, freshly squeezed
- ¼ C. red cabbage, sliced
- ¼ C. carrots, grated
- 1 lb. (454 g.) lean pork, ground
- ½ tsp. paprika
- 1 C. baby lettuce greens, mixed
- 2 small tomatoes, sliced
- 8 small low-sodium whole-wheat sandwich buns, cut in half

Directions

1. In a small bowl, combine the yogurt, 1 tbsp. mustard, lemon juice, cabbage, and carrots; mix and refrigerate.
2. In a medium bowl, combine the pork, remaining 1 tbsp. mustard, and paprika. Form into 8 small patties.

3. Put the patties into the air fryer basket. Air fry at 400ºF for 7–9 minutes, or until the patties register 165ºF as tested with a meat thermometer.

4. Assemble the burgers by placing some of the lettuce greens on a bun bottom. Top with a tomato slice, the patties, and the cabbage mixture. Add the bun top and serve immediately.

Nutrition

Calories: 473 kcal. **Fat:** 15 g. **Protein:** 35 g. **Carbs:** 51 g. **Fiber:** 8 g.

67. <u>Pork Taquitos in Air Fryer</u>

Preparation Time: 10 minutes **Cooking Time:** 20 minutes

Ingredients   (**Servings:** 10)

- 3 C. Pork tenderloin, cooked and shredded
- Cooking spray
- 2 and ½ C. mozzarella, shredded, fat-free
- 10 small tortillas
- Salsa for dipping
- 1 lime, juiced

Directions

1. Let the air fryer preheat to 380ºF.

2. Add lime juice to pork and mix well.

3. With a damp towel over the tortilla, microwave for 10 seconds to soften.

4. Add pork filling and cheese on top, in a tortilla, roll up the tortilla tightly.

5. Place tortillas on a greased foil pan.

6. Spray oil over tortillas. Cook for 7–10 minutes or until tortillas are golden brown, flip halfway through.

7. Serve with fresh salad.

Nutrition

Calories: 253 kcal. **Fat:** 18 g. **Carbs:** 10 g. **Protein:** 20 g.

68.　**Pork Chop and Broccoli**

Preparation Time: 20 minutes **Cooking Time:** 20 minutes

Ingredients　**(Servings:** 4)

- 2 C. broccoli florets
- 2 pcs. pork chop, bone-in
- ½ tsp. paprika
- 2 tbsp. avocado oil
- ½ tsp. garlic powder
- ½ tsp. onion powder
- 2 garlic cloves, crushed
- 1 tsp. salt, divided

Directions

1. Let the air fryer preheat to 350ºF. Spray the basket with cooking oil.

2. Add 1 tbsp. oil, onion powder, ½ tsp. salt, garlic powder, and paprika in a bowl mix well, rub this spice mix to the pork chop's sides.

3. Add pork chops to the air fryer basket and let it cook for 5 minutes.

4. In the meantime, add 1 tsp. oil, garlic, ½ teaspoon salt, and broccoli to a bowl and coat well.

5. Flip the pork chop and add the broccoli, let it cook for 5 more minutes.

6. Take out from the air fryer and serve.

Nutrition

Calories: 483 kcal. **Total Fat:** 20 g. **Carbohydrates:** 12 g. **Protein:** 23 g.

69.   <u>Pork Rind Nachos</u>

Preparation Time: 5 min **Cooking Time:** 5 min

Ingredients   (Servings: 2)

- 2 tbsp. pork rinds
- ¼ C. chicken, shredded and cooked
- ½ C. Monterey jack cheese, shredded
- ¼ C. jalapeños, sliced and pickled
- ¼ C. guacamole
- ¼ C. full-fat sour cream

Directions

- Put pork rinds in a 6 inches round baking pan. Fill with grilled chicken and Monterey cheese jack. Place the pan in the basket with the air fryer.
- Set the temperature to 370°F, and set the timer for 5 minutes
- Eat right away with jalapeños, guacamole, and sour cream.

Nutrition

Calories: 295 kcal. **Protein:** 30.1 g. **Fiber:** 1.2 g. **Carbohydrates:** 3.0 g.

70.   **Double Cheeseburger**

Preparation Time: 5 minutes **Cooking Time:** 18 minutes

Ingredients   (**Servings:** 1)

- 2 beef patties, pastured
- $\frac{1}{8}$ tsp. onion powder
- 2 slices mozzarella cheese, low fat
- $\frac{1}{8}$ tsp. black pepper, ground
- $\frac{1}{8}$ tsp. salt

Directions

1. Switch on the air fryer, insert the fryer basket, grease it with olive oil, then shut with its lid, set the fryer at 370ºF, and preheat for 5 minutes.
2. Meanwhile, season the patties well with onion powder, black pepper, and salt.
3. Open the fryer, add beef patties in it, close the lid and cook for 12 minutes until nicely golden and cooked, flipping the patties halfway through the frying.
4. Then top the patties with a cheese slice and continue cooking for 1 minute or until cheese melts.
5. Serve straight away.

Nutrition

Calories: 670 kcal. **Carbs:** 0 g. **Fat:** 50 g. **Protein:** 39 g.

71.   Beef Schnitzel

Preparation Time: 10 minutes **Cooking Time:** 15 minutes

Ingredients   (**Servings:** 1)

- 1 lean beef schnitzel
- 2 tbsp. Olive oil
- ¼ C. Breadcrumbs
- 1 egg
- 1 lemon, to serve

Directions

1. Let the air fryer heat to 356ºF.
2. In a big bowl, add breadcrumbs and oil, mix well until forms a crumbly mixture.
3. Dip beef steak in whisked egg and coat in breadcrumbs mixture.
4. Place the breaded beef in the air fryer and cook at 356ºF for 15 minutes or more until fully cooked through.
5. Take out from the air fryer and serve with the side of salad greens and lemon.

Nutrition

Calories: 340 kcal. **Proteins:** 20 g. **Carbs:** 14 g. **Fat:** 10 g.   **Fiber:** 7 g.

72.   <u>Hamburgers</u>

Preparation Time: 5 minutes **Cooking Time:** 13 minutes

Ingredients   (**Servings:** 4)

- 4 Buns
- 4 C. lean beef chuck, ground
- Salt to taste
- 4 slices any cheese
- Black Pepper, to taste

Directions

- Let the air fryer preheat to 350ºF.
- In a bowl, add lean ground beef, pepper, and salt. Mix well and form patties.
- Put them in the air fryer in 1 layer only, cook for 6 minutes, flip them halfway through. 1 minute before you take out the patties, add cheese on top.
- When cheese is melted, take it out from the air fryer.
- Add ketchup, any dressing to your buns, add tomatoes, and lettuce, and patties.
- Serve hot.

Nutrition

Calories: 520 kcal. **Carbohydrates:** 22 g. **Protein:** 31 g. **Fat:** 34 g.

73. <u>Beef Steak Kabobs With Vegetables</u>

Preparation Time: 30 minutes **Cooking Time:** 10 minutes

Ingredients   (**Servings:** 4)

- 2 tbsp. light soy sauce
- 4 C. lean beef chuck ribs, cut into 1-inch pcs
- ⅓ C. low-fat sour cream
- ½ onion
- 8 skewers (6 inches)
- 1 bell pepper

Directions

1. In a mixing bowl, add soy sauce and sour cream, mix well. Add the lean beef chunks, coat well, and let it marinate for half an hour or more.

2. Cut onion, bell pepper into 1-inch pieces. In water, soak skewers for 10 minutes.

3. Add onions, bell peppers, and beef on skewers; alternatively, sprinkle with black pepper.

4. Let it cook for 10 minutes in a preheated air fryer at 400ºF, flip halfway through.

5. Serve with yogurt dipping sauce.

Nutrition

Calories: 268 kcal. **Proteins:** 20 g. **Carbs:** 15 g. **Fat:** 10 g.

74. **Rib-Eye Steak**

Preparation Time: 5 minutes **Cooking Time:** 14 minutes

Ingredients   (**Servings:** 2)

- 2 medium-sized Lean rib-eye steaks
- Salt and black pepper, freshly ground, to taste

Directions

1. Let the air fry preheat at 400ºF. Pat dry steaks with paper towels.
2. Use any spice blend or just salt and pepper on steaks.
3. Generously on both sides of the steak.
4. Put steaks in the air fryer basket. Cook according to the rareness you want. Or cook for 14 minutes and flip after halftime.
5. Take out from the air fryer and let it rest for about 5 minutes.
6. Serve with a green salad.

Nutrition

Calories: 470 kcal. **Protein:** 45 g. **Fat:** 31 g. **Carbs:** 23 g.

75.   <u>Bunless Sloppy Joes</u>

Preparation Time: 15 minutes **Cooking Time:** 40 minutes

Ingredients   (**Servings:** 6)

- 6 small sweet potatoes
- 1 lb. (454 g) lean beef, ground
- 1 onion, finely chopped
- 1 carrot, finely chopped
- ¼ C. mushrooms, finely chopped
- ¼ C. red bell pepper, finely chopped
- 3 garlic cloves, minced
- 2 tsp. Worcestershire sauce
- 1 tbsp. white wine vinegar
- 1 (15-oz./425-g) can low-sodium tomato sauce
- 2 tbsp. tomato paste

Directions

1. Preheat the oven to 400ºF.
2. Place the sweet potatoes in a single layer in a baking dish. Bake for 25–40 minutes. depending on the size until they are soft and cooked through.
3. While the sweet potatoes are baking, in a large skillet, cook the beef over medium heat until it's browned, breaking it apart into small pieces as you stir.
4. Add the onion, carrot, mushrooms, bell pepper, and garlic, and sauté briefly for 1 minute.
5. Stir in the Worcestershire sauce, vinegar, tomato sauce, and tomato paste. Bring to a simmer, reduce the heat, and cook for 5 minutes for the flavours to meld.

Mark Spencer

6. Scoop ½ C. of the meat mixture on top of each baked potato and serve.

Nutrition

Calories: 372 kcal. **Fat:** 19 g. **Protein:** 16 g. **Fiber:** 6 g. **Sodium:** 161 mg.

7. Snack and Appetizers

Mark Spencer

Snack and Appetizers

76.   Kale Chips With Lemon Yogurt Sauce

Preparation Time: 10 minutes **Cooking Time:** 5 minutes

Ingredients   (**Servings:** 4)

- 1 C. plain Greek yogurt
- 3 tbsp. lemon juice, freshly squeezed
- 2 tbsp. honey mustard
- ½ tsp. oregano, dried
- 1 bunch curly kale
- 2 tbsp. olive oil
- ½ tsp. salt
- ⅛ tsp. pepper

Directions

1. In a small bowl, combine the yogurt, lemon juice, honey mustard, and oregano, and set aside.
2. Remove the stems and ribs from the kale with a sharp knife. Cut the leaves into 2- to 3-inch pieces.
3. Toss the kale with olive oil, salt, and pepper. Massage the oil into the leaves with your hands.
4. Air fry the kale in batches at 390ºF until crisp, about 5 minutes, shaking the basket once during cooking time. Serve with the yogurt sauce.

Nutrition

Calories: 155 kcal. **Fat:** 8 g. **Protein:** 8 g. **Carbs:** 13 g. **Fiber:** 1 g

77. Basil Pesto Bruschetta

Preparation Time: 10 minutes **Cooking Time:** 4–8 minutes

Ingredients   (**Servings:** 4)

- 8 slices French bread, ½ inch thick
- 2 tbsp. butter, softened
- 1 C. Mozzarella cheese, shredded
- ½ C. basil pesto
- 1 C. grape tomatoes, chopped
- 2 green onions, thinly sliced

Directions

1. Spread the bread with the butter and place butter-side up in the air fryer basket. Bake at 350ºF for 3–5 minutes or until the bread is light golden brown.
2. Remove the bread from the basket and top each piece with some of the cheese. Return to the basket in batches and bake until the cheese melts for about 1–3 minutes.
3. Meanwhile, combine the pesto, tomatoes, and green onions in a small bowl.
4. When the cheese has melted, remove the bread from the air fryer and place it on a serving plate. Top each slice with some of the pesto mixture and serve.

Nutrition

Calories: 463 kcal. **Fat:** 25 g. **Protein:** 19 g. **Carbs:** 41 g. **Fiber:** 3 g. **Sugar:** 2 g. **Sodium:** 822 mg.

78.   Phyllo Vegetable Triangles

Preparation Time: 15 minutes **Cooking Time:** 6–11 minutes

Ingredients   (**Servings:** 6)

- 3 tbsp. onion, minced
- 2 garlic cloves, minced
- 2 tbsp. carrot, grated
- 1 tsp. olive oil
- 3 tbsp. baby peas, frozen and thawed
- 2 tbsp. non-fat cream cheese, at room temperature
- 6 sheets phyllo dough, frozen and thawed
- Olive oil spray, for coating the dough

Directions

1. In a baking pan, combine the onion, garlic, carrot, and olive oil. Air fry at 390ºF for 2–4 minutes, or until the vegetables are crisp-tender. Transfer to a bowl.
2. Stir in the peas and cream cheese to the vegetable mixture. Let cool while you prepare the dough.
3. Lay 1 sheet of phyllo on a work surface and lightly spray with olive oil spray. Top with another sheet of phyllo. Repeat with the remaining 4 phyllo sheets; you'll have 3 stacks with 2 layers each. Cut each stack lengthwise into 4 strips (12 strips total).
4. Place a scant 2 tsp. of the filling near the bottom of each strip. Bring one corner up over the filling to make a triangle; continue folding the triangles over, as you would fold a flag. Seal the edge with a bit of water. Repeat with the remaining strips and filling.

5. Air fry the triangles, in 2 batches, for 4–7 minutes, or until golden brown. Serve.

Nutrition

Calories: 67 kcal. **Fat:** 2 g. **Protein:** 2 g. **Carbs:** 11 g. **Fiber:** 1 g. **Sodium:** 121 mg.

79. Red Cabbage and Mushroom Pot Stickers

Preparation Time: 12 minutes **Cooking Time:** 11–18 minutes

Ingredients Servings: Makes 12 pot stickers

- 1 C. red cabbage, shredded
- ¼ C. button mushrooms, chopped
- ¼ C. carrot, grated
- 2 tbsp. onion, minced
- 2 garlic cloves, minced
- 2 tsp. fresh ginger, grated
- 12 gyoza/pot sticker wrappers
- 2 ½ tsp. olive oil, divided

Directions

1. In a baking pan, combine the red cabbage, mushrooms, carrot, onion, garlic, and ginger. Add 1 tbsp. water. Place in the air fryer and bake at 370ºF for 3–6 minutes, until the vegetables are crisp-tender. Drain and set aside.

2. Working one at a time, place the pot sticker wrappers on a work surface. Top each wrapper with a scant 1 tbsp. of the filling. Fold half

of the wrapper over the other half to form a half-circle. Dab 1 edge with water and press both edges together.

3. To the baking pan, add 1 ¼ tsp. olive oil. Put half of the pot stickers, seam-side up, in the pan. Air fry for 5 minutes, or until the bottoms are light golden brown. Add 1 tbsp. water and return the pan to the air fryer.

4. Air fry for 4–6 minutes more, or until hot. Repeat with the remaining pot stickers, remaining 1¼ tsp. oil, and another tbsp. water. Serve immediately.

Nutrition

Calories: 88 kcal. **Fat:** 3 g. **Protein:** 2 g. **Carbs:** 14 g. **Fiber:** 1 g. **Sodium:** 58 mg.

80. <u>**Garlic Roasted Mushrooms**</u>

Preparation Time: 3 minutes **Cooking Time:** 22–27 minutes

Ingredients   (**Servings:** 4)

- 16 garlic cloves, peeled
- 2 tsp. olive oil, divided
- 16 button mushrooms
- ½ tsp. marjoram, dried
- 1/8 tsp. black pepper, freshly ground
- 1 tbsp. white wine or low-sodium vegetable broth

Directions

1. In a baking pan, mix the garlic with 1 tsp. olive oil. Roast in the air fryer at 350ºF for 12 minutes.

2. Add the mushrooms, marjoram, and pepper. Stir to coat. Drizzle with the remaining 1 tsp. olive oil and white wine.

3. Return to the air fryer and roast for 10–15 minutes more, or until the mushrooms and garlic cloves are tender. Serve.

Nutrition

Calories: 128 kcal. **Fat:** 4 g. **Protein:** 13 g. **Carbs:** 17 g. **Fiber:** 4 g. **Sugar:** 8 g. **Sodium:** 20 mg.

81. Baked Spicy Chicken Meatballs

Preparation Time: 10 minutes **Cooking Time:** 11–14 minutes

Ingredients Servings: Makes 24 meatballs

- 1 medium red onion, minced
- 2 garlic cloves, minced
- 1 jalapeño pepper, minced
- 2 tsp. olive oil
- 3 tbsp. almonds, ground
- 1 egg
- 1 tsp. thyme, dried
- 1 lb. (454 g) chicken breast, ground

Directions

1. In a baking pan, combine the red onion, garlic, jalapeño, and olive oil. Bake at 400ºF for 3–4 minutes, or until the vegetables are crisp-tender. Transfer to a medium bowl.

2. Mix in the almonds, egg, and thyme to the vegetable mixture. Add the chicken and mix until just combined.

3. Form the chicken mixture into about 24 (1-inch) balls. Bake the meatballs, in batches, for 8 to 10 minutes, until the chicken reaches an internal temperature of 165ºF on a meat thermometer.

Nutrition

Calories: 186 kcal. **Fat:** 7 g. **Protein:** 29 g. **Carbs:** 5 g. **Fiber:** 1 g. **Sodium:** 55 mg.

82.   Crispy Parmesan Cauliflower

Preparation Time: 12 minutes **Cooking Time:** 14–17 minutes

Ingredients Servings: Makes 20 cauliflower bites

- 4 C. cauliflower florets
- 1 C. whole-wheat bread crumbs
- 1 tsp. coarse sea salt or kosher salt
- ¼ C. Parmesan cheese, grated
- ¼ C. butter
- ¼ C. mild hot sauce
- Olive oil spray

Directions

1. Place a parchment liner in the air fryer basket.

2. Cut the cauliflower florets in half and set them aside.

3. In a small bowl, mix the bread crumbs, salt, and Parmesan; set aside.

4. In a small microwave-safe bowl, combine the butter and hot sauce. Heat in the microwave until the butter is melted, about 15 seconds. Whisk.

5. Holding the stems of the cauliflower florets, dip them in the butter mixture to coat. Shake off any excess mixture.

6. Dredge the dipped florets in the bread crumb mixture, then put them in the air fryer basket. There's no need for a single layer; just toss them all in there.

7. Spray the cauliflower lightly with olive oil and air fry at 350ºF for 14–17 minutes, shaking the basket a few times throughout the cooking process. The florets are done when they are lightly browned and crispy. Serve warm.

Nutrition

Calories: 106 kcal. **Fat:** 6 g. **Protein:** 3 g. **Carbs:** 10 g. **Fiber:** 1 g.

83.   <u>**Cream Cheese Stuffed Jalapeños**</u>

Preparation Time: 12 minutes **Cooking Time:** 6–8 minutes

Ingredients Servings: Makes 10 poppers

- 8 oz. (227 g.) cream cheese, at room temperature
- 1 C. whole-wheat bread crumbs, divided
- 2 tbsp. fresh parsley, minced
- 1 tsp. chili powder
- 10 jalapeño peppers, halved and seeded

Directions

1. In a small bowl, combine the cream cheese, ½ C. bread crumbs, the parsley, and the chili powder. Whisk to combine.

2. Stuff the cheese mixture into the jalapeños.

3. Sprinkle the tops of the stuffed jalapeños with the remaining ½ C. bread crumbs.

4. Place in the air fryer basket and air fry at 360ºF for 6–8 minutes, until the peppers are softened, and the cheese is melted. Serve warm.

Nutrition

Calories: 344 kcal. **Fat:** 16 g. **Protein:** 6 g. **Carbs:** 19 g. **Fiber:** 2 g. **Sugar:** 4 g. **Sodium:** 341 mg.

84.   <u>Smoked Salmon Dip</u>

Preparation Time: 10 minutes **Cooking Time:** 7 minutes

Ingredients   (**Servings:** 6)

- 1 (6-oz./170-g) can salmon, boneless, skinless
- 8 oz. (227 g) cream cheese, softened
- 1 tbsp. liquid smoke (optional)
- ¹/¹/₃ C. pecans, chopped
- ½ C. green onions, chopped
- 1 tsp. kosher salt (or less if the salmon contains salt)
- 1 to 2 tsp. black pepper
- ¼ tsp. paprika, smoked, for garnish
- Cucumber and celery slices, cocktail rye bread, or crackers

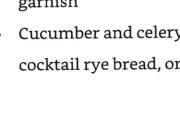

Directions

1. In a baking pan, combine the salmon, softened cream cheese, liquid smoke (if using), pecans, ¼ C. green onions, salt, and pepper. Stir until well combined.

2. Place the pan in the air fryer basket. Bake at 400ºF for 7 minutes, or until the cheese melts.

3. Sprinkle with the paprika and top with the remaining ¼ C. green onions. Serve with sliced vegetables, cocktail breads, or crackers.

Nutrition

Calories: 235 kcal. **Fat:** 19 g. **Protein:** 13 g. **Carbs:** 3 g.

85.   Simple Corn Tortilla Chips

Preparation Time: 5 minutes **Cooking Time:** 10 minutes

Ingredients   (**Servings:** 4)

- 4 (6-inch) corn tortillas
- 1 tbsp. canola oil
- ¼ tsp. kosher salt
- Stack corn tortillas, cut in half and then slice into thirds.

Directions

1. Spray the air fryer basket with cooking spray, then brush the tortillas with canola oil and place them in the basket. Air fry at 360ºF for 5 minutes.

2. Pause the fryer to shake the basket, then air fry for 3–5 more minutes or until golden brown and crispy.

3. Remove the chips from the fryer and place them on a plate lined with a paper towel. Sprinkle the kosher salt on top before serving warm.

Nutrition

Calories: 72 kcal. **Fat:** 4 g. **Protein:** 1 g. **Carbs:** 8 g. **Fiber:** 1 g. **Sodium:** 79 mg.

86. **Tomato Dip**

Preparation Time: 10 minutes **Cooking Time:** 20 minutes

Ingredients   (**Servings:** 4)

- 1 lb. tomatoes
- Salt and black pepper to the taste
- 2 tbsp. avocado oil
- 2 tbsp. balsamic vinegar
- 1 tbsp. basil, chopped
- 1 C. heavy cream

Directions

1. In your air fryer's basket, combine the tomatoes with the oil and the other ingredients except for the cream, toss and cook at 220ºF for 20 minutes.
2. Peel and transfer the tomatoes to a blender, add the cream, pulse, divide into bowls and serve.

Nutrition

Calories: 135 kcal. **Fat:** 12.2 g. **Fiber:** 1.7 g. **Carbs:** 5.7 g. **Protein**: 1.7 g.

87.   Air Fryer Egg Rolls

Preparation Time: 10 minute **Cooking Time:** 20 minutes

Ingredients   (**Servings:** 3)

- ½ bag Coleslaw mix
- ½ onion
- ½ tsp. Salt
- ½ C. mushrooms
- 2 C. Lean ground pork
- 1 stalk celery
- 1/3 C. Wrappers (egg roll)

Directions

1. Put a skillet over medium flame, add onion and lean ground pork and cook for 5–7 minutes.
2. Add coleslaw mixture, salt, mushrooms, and celery to skillet and cook for almost 5 minutes.
3. Lay egg roll wrapper flat and add filling (⅓ C.), roll it up, seal with water.
4. Spray with oil the rolls.
5. Put in the air fryer for 6–8 minutes at 400ºF, flipping once halfway through.
6. Serve hot.

Nutrition

Calories: 245 kcal. **Fat:** 10 g. **Net Carbs:** 9 g. **Protein:** 11 g.

8. Desserts

Desserts

88.   Tasty Banana Cake

Preparation Time: 40 minutes **Cooking Time:** 30 minutes

Ingredients   (**Servings:** 4)

- 1 tbsp. butter, soft
- 1 egg
- ⅓ C. brown sugar
- 2 tbsp. honey
- 1 banana
- 1 C. white flour
- 1 tbsp. baking powder
- ½ tbsp. cinnamon powder
- Cooking spray

Directions

1. Spurt cake pan with cooking spray.
2. Mix in butter with honey, sugar, banana, cinnamon, egg, flour, and baking powder in a bowl, then beat.
3. Empty mix in a cake pan with cooking spray put into the air fryer, and cook at 350°F for 30 minutes.
4. Allow cooling, slice.
5. Serve.

Nutrition

Calories: 145 kcal. **Fat:** 16 g. **Carbohydrates:** 9 g. **Proteins:** 4 g.

89.   Air Fried Bananas

Preparation Time: 10 minutes   **Cooking Time:** 14 minutes

Ingredients   **(Servings:** 4)

- 3 tbsp. butter
- 2 eggs
- 8 bananas
- ½ C. corn flour
- 3 tbsp. cinnamon sugar
- 1 C. panko

Directions

1. Warm up the pan with the butter over medium heat, put panko, mix, and cook for 4 minutes, then move to a bowl.
2. Spin each in flour, panko, egg blend, assemble them in the air fryer's basket, grime with cinnamon sugar, and cook at 280°F for 10 minutes.
3. Serve immediately.

Nutrition

Calories: 166 kcal. **Fat:** 11 g. **Carbohydrates:** 9 g. **Proteins:** 4 g.

90.   Cocoa Cake

Preparation Time: 10 minutes **Cooking Time:** 22 minutes

Ingredients   **(Servings:** 4)

- 1 tbsp. butter
- 3 eggs
- 3 oz. sugar
- 1 tbsp. cocoa powder
- 3 oz. flour
- ½ tbsp. lemon juice

Directions

1. Mix in 1 tbsp. butter with cocoa powder in a bowl and beat.
2. Mix in the rest of the butter with eggs, flour, sugar, and lemon juice in another bowl, blend well and move half into a cake pan
3. Put half of the cocoa blend, spread, add the rest of the butter layer, and crest with remaining cocoa.
4. Put into the air fryer and cook at 360°F for 17 minutes.
5. Allow cooling before slicing.
6. Serve.

Nutrition

Calories: 139 kcal. **Fat:** 11 g. **Carbohydrates:** 2 g. **Proteins:** 4 g.

91. Apple Bread

Preparation Time: 10 minutes **Cooking Time:** 46 minutes

Ingredients **(Servings: 6)**

- 3 C. apples
- ½ C. sugar
- 1 tbsp. vanilla
- 2 eggs
- 1 tbsp. apple pie spice
- 2 C. white flour
- 1 tbsp. baking powder
- 1 stick butter
- 1 C. water

Directions

1. Mix in egg with 1 butter stick, sugar, and apple pie spice, then turn using a mixer.
2. Put apples and mix well.
3. Mix baking powder with flour in another bowl and turn.
4. Blend the 2 mixtures, turn, and move them to the springform pan.
5. Get springform pan into the air fryer, and cook at 320°F for 40 minutes
6. Slice.
7. Serve.

Nutrition

Calories: 144 kcal. **Fat:** 16 g. **Carbohydrates:** 2 g. **Proteins:** 9 g.

92. <u>Banana Bread</u>

Preparation Time: 10 minutes   **Cooking Time:** 42 minutes

Ingredients   **(Servings:** 6)

- ¾ C. sugar
- ⅓ C. butter
- 1 tbsp. vanilla extract
- 1 egg
- 2 bananas

- 1-½ C. flour
- ½ tbsp. baking soda
- ⅓ C. milk
- 1-½ tbsp. tartar cream
- Cooking spray

- 1 tbsp. baking powder

Directions

1. Mix in milk with cream of tartar, vanilla, egg, sugar, bananas, and butter in a bowl and turn whole.
2. Mix in flour with baking soda and baking powder.
3. Blend the 2 mixtures, mix well, move into the oiled pan with cooking spray, put into the air fryer, and cook at 320°F for 40 minutes.
4. Remove bread, allow to cool, slice.
5. Serve.

Nutrition

Calories: 184 kcal. **Fat:** 14 g. **Carbohydrates:** 5 g. **Proteins:** 4 g.

93. Crispy Apples

Preparation Time: 10 minutes **Cooking Time:** 10–15 minutes

Ingredients   (**Servings:** 4)

- 2 tbsp. cinnamon powder
- 5 apples
- ½ tbsp. nutmeg powder
- 1 tbsp. maple syrup
- ½ C. water
- 4 tbsp. butter
- ¼ C. flour
- ¾ C. oats
- ¼ C. brown sugar

Directions

1. Get the apples in a pan, put them in nutmeg, maple syrup, cinnamon, and water.

2. Mix in butter with flour, sugar, salt, and oat, put a spoonful of the blend over apples, get into the air fryer, and cook at 350°F for 10 minutes.

3. Serve while warm.

Nutrition

Calories: 169 kcal. **Fat:** 17 g. **Carbohydrates:** 2 g. **Proteins:** 2 g.

94.   <u>Ginger Cheesecake</u>

Preparation Time: 2 hours and 30 minutes   **Cooking Time:** 20–25 minutes

Ingredients   (**Servings:** 6)

- 2 tbsp. butter
- ½ C. ginger cookies
- 16 oz. cream cheese
- 2 eggs
- ½ C. sugar
- 1 tbsp. rum
- ½ tbsp. vanilla extract
- ½ tbsp. nutmeg

Directions

1. Spread pan with the butter and sprinkle cookie crumbs on the bottom.
2. Whisk cream cheese with rum, vanilla, nutmeg, and eggs mix well and sprinkle the cookie crumbs.
3. Put in the air fryer, and cook at 340°F for 20 minutes.
4. Allow cheesecake to cool in the fridge for 2 hours before slicing.
5. Serve.

Nutrition

Calories: 195 kcal. **Fat:** 18 g. **Carbohydrates:** 2 g. **Proteins:** 4 g.

95.   Cocoa Cookies

Preparation Time: 10 minutes   **Cooking Time:** 15–20 minutes

Ingredients **(Servings:** 12)

- 6 oz. coconut oil
- 6 eggs
- 3 oz. cocoa powder
- 2 tbsp. vanilla
- ½ tbsp. baking powder
- 4 oz. cream cheese
- 2 tbsp. sugar

Directions

1. Mix in eggs with coconut oil, baking powder, sugar, cocoa powder, cream cheese, vanilla in a blender and sway and turn using a mixer.

2. Get it into a lined baking dish and into the fryer at 320°F and bake for 14 minutes.

3. Split cookie sheet into rectangles.

4. Serve.

Nutrition

Calories: 185 kcal. **Fat:** 19 g. **Carbohydrates:** 6 g. **Proteins:** 4 g.

96.   Chocolate Cookies

Preparation Time: 10 minutes   **Cooking Time:** 26 minutes

Ingredients   (**Servings:** 12)

- 1 tbsp. vanilla extract
- ½ C. butter
- 1 egg
- 2 tbsp. sugar
- 2 C. flour
- ½ C. chocolate chips, unsweetened

Directions

1. Warm pan with butter over medium heat, turn and cook for 1 minute.
2. Mix in egg with sugar and vanilla extract in a bowl and mix well.
3. Put flour, melted butter, and half of the chocolate chips, and turn.
4. Move to a pan, sprinkle the remaining chocolate chips over, put in the fryer at 330°F, and bake for 25 minutes.
5. Serve slices when cold.

Nutrition

Calories: 147 kcal. **Fat:** 20 g. **Carbohydrates:** 4 g. **Proteins:** 3 g.

97.   **Lime Cheesecake**

Preparation Time: 4 hours and 14 minutes   **Cooking Time:** 5 minutes

Ingredients   (Servings: 10)

- 2 tbsp. butter
- 1 tbsp. sugar
- 4 oz. flour
- ¼ C. coconut

For the filling:

- 1 lb. cream cheese
- Zest from 1 lime
- Juice from 1 lime
- 2 C. hot water
- 2 sachets lime jelly

Directions

1. Mix coconut with flour, sugar, and butter in a bowl, mix well and compress mix to the bottom of the pan.
2. Get hot water in a bowl, put jelly sachets, and mix till it melts.
3. Get cream cheese in a bowl, put the lime juice, zest, and jelly and mix well.
4. Get mix on the crust, rub, put in the air fryer, and cook at 300°F for 4 minutes.
5. Cool in the fridge for 4 hours
6. Serve.

Nutrition

Calories: 199 kcal. **Fat:** 11 g. **Carbohydrates:** 8 g. **Proteins:** 5 g.

98.   Air Fryer Thumbprint Cookies

Preparation Time: 15 minutes **Cooking Time:** 8 minutes

Ingredients   (Servings: 10)

- 1 tsp. baking powder
- 1 C. almond flour
- 3 tbsp. natural low-calorie sweetener
- 1 large egg
- 3-½ tbsp. raspberry preserves (reduced-sugar)
- 4 tbsp. cream cheese, softened

Directions

1. In a large bowl, add egg, baking powder, flour, sweetener, and cream cheese, mix well until a dough (wet) forms.
2. Chill the dough in the fridge for almost 20 minutes, until dough is cool enough
3. And then form into balls.
4. Let the air fryer preheat to 400°F, add the parchment paper to the air fryer basket.
5. Make 10 balls from the dough and put them in the prepared air fryer basket.
6. With your clean hands, make an indentation from your thumb in the center of every cookie. Add 1 tsp. of the raspberry preserve in the thumb hole.
7. Bake in the air fryer for 7 minutes or until light golden brown to your liking.
8. Let the cookies cool completely in the parchment paper for almost 15 minutes, or they will fall apart.

9. Serve with tea and enjoy.

Nutrition

Calories: 111.6 kcal. **Fat:** 8.6 g. **Carbohydrates:** 9.1 g. **Proteins:** 3.7 g.

99. <u>**Air Fryer Apple Fritter**</u>

Preparation Time: 9 minutes **Cooking Time:** 15 minutes

Ingredients **(Servings:** 3)

- ½ apple (Pink Lady Apple or Honey crisp) peeled, finely chopped
- ½ C. all-purpose flour
- 1 tsp. baking powder
- ¼ tsp. kosher salt
- ½ tsp. cinnamon, ground
- 2 tbsp. brown sugar or sugar alternative
- $\frac{1}{8}$ tsp. nutmeg, ground
- 3 tbsp. Greek yogurt (fat-free)
- 1 tbsp. butter

For the glaze:

- 2 tbsp. powdered sugar
- ½ tbsp. water

Directions

1. In a big mixing bowl, add baking powder, nutmeg, brown sugar (or alternative), flour, cinnamon, and salt. Mix it well,
2. With the help of a knife, slice the butter until crumbly. It should look like wet sand.
3. Add the chopped apple and coat well, then add fat-free Greek yogurt.
4. Keep stirring or tossing everything together, until a crumbly dough forms.

5. Put the dough on a clean surface and with your hands, knead it into a ball form.

6. Flatten the dough in an oval shape about a ½-inch thick. It is okay, even if it's not the perfect size or shape.

7. Spray the basket of the air fryer with cooking spray generously. Put the dough in the air fry for 12–14 minutes at 375ºF cook until light golden brown.

8. For making the glaze mix, the ingredients, and with the help of a brush, pour over the apple fritter when it comes out from the air fryer.

9. Slice and serve after cooling for 5 minutes.

Nutrition

Calories: 200 kcal. **Fat:** 12 g. **Carbohydrates:** 14 g. **Proteins:** 9.8 g.

100.   **Berry Cheesecake**

Preparation Time: 9 minutes **Cooking Time:** 51 minutes

Ingredients (**Servings:** 8)

- ½ C. raspberries
- 2 blocks cream cheese, softened, (8 oz.)
- 1 tsp. raspberry or vanilla extract
- ¼ C. strawberries
- 2 eggs
- ¼ C. blackberries
- 1 C. and 2 tbsp. sugar alternative of confectioner sweetener

Directions

1. In a big mixing bowl, whip the sugar-alternative confectioner sweetener and cream cheese, mix whip until smooth and creamy.

2. Then add in the raspberry or vanilla extract and eggs, again mix well.

3. In a food processor or a blender, pulse the berries and fold into the cream cheese mix with 2 extra tbsp. sweetener.

4. Take a springform pan and spray the oil generously, pour in the mixture.

5. Cook for 10 minutes at 400°F then set the temperature down to 300°F and cook for another 40 minutes.

6. Take out from the air fryer and cool a bit before chilling in the fridge.

7. Keep in the fridge for 2–4 hours.

Nutrition

Calories: 225 kcal. **Fat:** 17 g. **Carbohydrates:** 18 g. **Proteins:** 12 g.

101. Sugar-Free Air Fried Carrot Cake

Preparation Time: 14 minutes **Cooking Time:** 41 minutes

Ingredients   (**Servings:** 8)

- 1 ¼ C. all-purpose flour
- 1 tsp. pumpkin pie spice
- 1 tsp. baking powder
- ¾ C. Splenda
- 2 C. carrots, grated
- 2 eggs
- ½ tsp. baking soda
- ¾ C. canola oil

Directions

1. Let the air fryer preheat to 350°F. Spray the pan with oil spray.
2. And add flour over that.
3. In a bowl, combine the baking powder, flour, pumpkin pie spice, and baking soda.
4. In another bowl, mix the eggs, oil, and sugar alternative. Now combine the dry to wet ingredients.
5. Add half of the dry ingredients first mix and the other half of the dry mixture.
6. Add the grated carrots.
7. Add the butter to the greased cake pan.
8. Let it air fry for 30 minutes, and do not let the top too brown.
9. If the top is browning, add a piece of foil over the top of the cake.
10. Air fry it until a toothpick comes out clean, 35–40 minutes in total.

Nutrition

Calories: 287 kcal. **Fat:** 22 g.   **Carbohydrates:** 19 g.   **Proteins:** 4 g.

Mark Spencer

Meal Plan 28 Days

Days	Breakfast	Lunch	Dinner
1	Chicken and Zucchini Omelette	Chicken Wings	Double Cheeseburger
2	Lemony Raspberries Bowls	Air Fryer Shrimp Scampi	Pork Spare Ribs
3	Scrambled Eggs	Crispy Fish Sandwiches	Cajun Shrimp in Air Fryer
4	Mushroom Cheese Salad	Chicken Wings With Curry	Basil-Parmesan Crusted Salmon
5	Tuna and Spring Onions Salad	Lemon Pepper Chicken	Cilantro Lime Shrimps
6	Shrimp Frittata	Salmon on Bed of Fennel and Carrot	Parmesan Garlic Crusted Salmon
7	Zucchini Squash Mix	Buffalo Chicken Hot Wings	Lemon Pepper Chicken
8	Onion Omelette	Tilapia	Crispy Fish Sticks in Air Fryer

9	Mushrooms and Cheese Spread	Parmesan Garlic Crusted Salmon	Chicken Wings With Curry
10	Chicken Omelette	Fish and Seafood	Tomato Basil Scallops
11	Shrimp Sandwiches	Air Fryer Fish and Chips	Scallops With Green Vegetables
12	Breakfast Pea Tortilla	Garlic Rosemary Grilled Prawns	Chicken Meatballs
13	Shrimp Frittata	Tex-Mex Salmon Stir-Fry	Garlic Rosemary Grilled Prawns
14	Breakfast Pea Tortilla	Pork Chop and Broccoli	Crispy Fish Sandwiches
15	Garlic Potatoes with Bacon	Air-Fried Crumbed Fish	Fish and Seafood
16	Mushrooms and Cheese Spread	Crispy Fish Sticks in Air Fryer	Lemon Pepper Shrimp in Air Fryer
17	Garlic Potatoes with Bacon	Roasted Vegetable Chicken Salad	Pork Burgers With Red Cabbage Slaw

18	Lemony Raspberries Bowls	Scallops With Green Vegetables	Rib-Eye Steak
19	Sweet Nuts Butter	Chicken Meatballs	BBQ Pork Ribs
20	Tuna and Spring Onions Salad	Salmon Cakes	Tex-Mex Salmon Stir-Fry
21	Tuna Sandwiches	Double Cheeseburger	Pork Taquitos in Air Fryer
22	Shrimp Sandwiches	Shrimp Scampi	Salmon Cakes
23	Tuna Sandwiches	Pork Burgers With Red Cabbage Slaw	Shrimp Scampi
24	Zucchini Squash Mix	Salmon Cakes in Air Fryer	Lemon Garlic Shrimp in Air Fryer
25	Sweet Nuts Butter	Stuffed Chicken	Air Fryer Salmon With Maple Soy Glaze
26	Chicken Omelette	Chicken in Tomato Juice	Air Fryer Fish and Chips

27	Scrambled Eggs	Air Fryer Salmon With Maple Soy Glaze	Pork Rind Nachos
28	Onion Omelette	Pork Taquitos in Air Fryer	Grilled Salmon With Lemon

Conclusion

Diabetes has a huge impact on our society today. Among the chronic diseases, diabetes is spreading more and more with the numbers that are constantly increasing.

Knowing how to keep under control the disease is very important to continue living life without worrying about complications or experiencing any major health problems. One way to do it is to understand how much your diet can affect your blood sugar levels. There are small things you can do in the kitchen that can not only help with managing your diabetes but also benefit your overall health.

One popular today and versatile way is cooking your food using an Air Fryer. These appliances allow you to fry food without all of the side effects that come along with frying or deep frying.

A key aspect is to work more on "prevention", reducing the chance for patients to be affected by this disease. The Air Fryer is not the solution. It is one step towards a healthy and balanced lifestyle. Start being positive with simple steps, focus on your diet, find a sport you like, and remember that you are not alone.

As my father did, I am sure everyone can prepare simple dishes when you are on your own, you are going to have someone for dinner or even planning a big party. This cookbook is not only for those with diabetes but for the whole family.

Measurement Conversions

VOLUME EQUIVALENTS (DRY)

US STANDARD	METRIC (APPROXIMATE)
1/8 teaspoon	0.5 mL
1/4 teaspoon	1 mL
1/2 teaspoon	2 mL
3/4 teaspoon	4 mL
1 teaspoon	5 mL
1 tablespoon	15 mL
1/4 cup	59 mL
1/2 cup	118 mL
3/4 cup	177 mL
1 cup	235 mL
2 cups	475 mL
3 cups	700 mL
4 cups	1 L

VOLUME EQUIVALENTS (LIQUID)

US STANDARD	US STANDARD (OUNCES)	METRIC (APPROXIMATE)
2 tablespoons	1 fl.oz.	30 mL
1/4 cup	2 fl.oz.	60 mL
1/2 cup	4 fl.oz.	120 mL
1 cup	8 fl.oz.	240 mL
1 1/2 cup	12 fl.oz.	355 mL
2 cups or 1 pint	16 fl.oz.	475 mL
4 cups or 1 quart	32 fl.oz.	1 L
1 gallon	128 fl.oz.	4 L

TEMPERATURE EQUIVALENTS

FAHRENHEIT (F)	CELSIUS (C) (APPROXIMATE)
225 °F	107 °C
250 °F	120 °C
275 °F	135 °C
300 °F	150 °C
325 °F	160 °C
350 °F	180 °C
375 °F	190 °C
400 °F	205 °C
425 °F	220 °C
450 °F	235 °C
475 °F	245 °C
500 °F	260 °C

WEIGHT EQUIVALENTS

US STANDARD	METRIC (APPROXIMATE)
1 ounce	28 g
2 ounces	57 g
5 ounces	142 g
10 ounces	284 g
15 ounces	425 g
16 ounces (1 pound)	455 g
1.5 pounds	680 g
2 pounds	907 g

Index

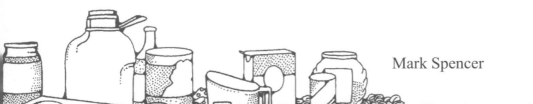

Notes

Made in the USA
Thornton, CO
02/03/24 05:01:33

2a2f95b3-4db5-441a-93af-2ed240382dabR01